THE LOST ART OF
COMMUNICATION
INTELLIGENCE

To Nicky
With Love
Sharon. xxx
3.5.23

THE LOST ART OF
COMMUNICATION
INTELLIGENCE

THE DEFINITIVE GUIDE TO 21st CENTURY COMMUNICATION

SHARON CHRISTIAAN

For my twin daughters Monopoly and Minerva, who have been my constant source of inspiration and strength. You have given me the confidence 'to dare to be vulnerable' and follow my dreams.

ABOUT THE AUTHOR

S haron Christiaan is an expert in communication, decision-making and judgement. She draws on her experience as a lawyer, internal communication specialist, compliance officer and behavioural scientist. Today she is making a name for herself as the leading authority in Communication Intelligence. Sharon believes in the power of inspiring, empowering and uniting.

www.sharonchristiaan.co.uk
Connect with Sharon on LinkedIn
https://www.linkedin.com/in/slchristiaan/

AUTHOR'S NOTE

The recent pandemic has thrown the entire world into a communication paradigm shift, leading the vast majority of humankind to rapidly upgrade their communication skills to incorporate digital platforms and artificial intelligence.

The designers and corporations behind the digital platforms and artificial intelligence incorporate science and data analysis to maximise their effectiveness.

The current Communication Revolution has led to behavioural and psychological ramifications the world has never experienced in the history of humankind.

If you find yourself feeling out of your depth or unsure of what communication technique you should employ, this book should provide guidance.

Once humankind becomes aware of the actual underlying challenges in communication and a critical mass gains a conscious understanding of Communication Intelligence, society will take a quantum leap into a whole new way of life.

I've written the following story as guidance towards this new understanding. If you feel it touches you and believe it makes a difference in your life, then pass it on to another and help reach the critical mass in Communication Intelligence.

CHAPTER 1

FRIDAY, 11:30 A.M.

I arrived at the Queens Lane Coffee House in Oxford, which is just around the corner from Oxford University, and chose a seat near the window, a little back from the passing trade. Leaning back in my chair, I sipped on my vanilla latte, waiting for Ruben, totally in awe of the fact this café was first established in 1654. I couldn't help but wonder about all the amazing people and conversations that had taken place in this tiny café. I contemplated the secrets, dramas, and insights shared in this very spot. Ruben, I knew, would be late, even though we hadn't seen each other in over fifteen years—some things never change. I was intrigued to know what he wanted to discuss. We'd reconnected on LinkedIn two months ago. He seemed keen to meet up, and it had to be in person. But why? We'd lost contact after I'd left Australia and moved back to London.

It was another grey, cloudy day in the middle of winter, with only distant dreams of spring on the horizon. How I longed for the Australian summer and barefoot walks along the beach. Ruben and I had spent many a joyful sunset walking along remote beaches in Sydney, planning our future. We'd known each other since we were seven, our families had holidayed together. I wondered if Ruben was as handsome and charming as ever with his devilish smile and twinkle in his eye. Would I still recognise him? What did he mention in his message—something about helping him locate a lost diary or something?

"I'm only here on a quick stopover before I head to Amsterdam," he said.

"Can we catch up for a sneaky coffee? I have a fascinating piece of information that could truly change the way people communicate. I've heard it will create a massive paradigm shift in cultural awareness and transform relationships. It aligns relationships with outcomes."

Just my kind of intrigue and problem solving, something I'd love to sink my teeth into. What did Ruben mean by that?

The café was starting to fill up and get noisy. Where was Ruben? Why wasn't he answering his phone or replying to my messages? He's got ten minutes and I'm leaving; I'm far too busy to be messed around by Ruben—again!

Just then, he strolled in amongst a small group of tourists taking selfies.

"Hey babe," he said, giving me that familiar cheeky look with his hypnotic blue eyes. "Good to see neither you nor your time-keeping has changed."

"Ditto!" I noticed he still wore his irresistible aftershave and had a few grey hairs that just made him look even more distinguished and debonair. Why is it that time is so much kinder to men than women? I thought.

"Sorry for the delay. I decided to quickly say hi to my old university professor and got side-tracked by some commotion in the psychology department," Ruben said. "It was odd—I mentioned to Vlad that I was searching for an old diary written in Holland by unknown prisoners in a transit camp during World War Two. Someone must have overheard our conversation because suddenly I heard running down the corridor and saw a group of people look at me, then slam a door shut. Anyway, let's order. I don't have much time. I've got another meeting in two hours."

Great, I thought, I've got a million and one things to do, and the traffic back to London is horrendous this time of day.

A waitress approached and took our lunch order. We had a general chit chat while we waited for our food to arrive. I must have constantly been looking at my watch and phone for messages. Ruben leaned forwarded and broke my spell, placing his hand on my arm and looking into my eyes.

"OK, out with it, Iris, I know you too well. What's going on? You've shifted into corporate mode. Untouchable and professional. You've put up your barrier and withdrawn into isolation camp again."

I looked into my latte, trying desperately to change the subject. I didn't like talking about myself or my personal life. Over the years since my husband Arthur died, I'd withdrawn into my self-imposed protective shell. Trying to be both Mum and Dad to the twins whilst working as an immigration lawyer and spending my days fulfilling other people's dreams had taken its toll. Year-on-year, without me realising it, my isolation had slowly chipped away at my soul. I was so determined to help other people transform their life, whilst being the best parent to my children, that somehow, I'd lost myself along the way.

"Come on out with it—it's me. We've always been honest with each other. Remember how we told each other our darkest secrets whilst skipping stones on the lake, making plans about our future whilst climbing to the top of the highest tree and constantly getting into trouble for raiding the pantry before dinner?"

"Well, to be honest, I'm at crossroads in my life," I confessed. "The girls are getting older and more independent, and I'm just unsure what to do next. I've lost touch with who I am." I sighed. "My life has become a tedious process of the same daily grind—papers in, papers out and repeat. I'm great at creating systems, processes and procedures. I'm excellent at finding solutions to other people's problems, but I'm embarrassed to say relationships are not my strong point."

"Sounds to me like you need a break from your routine and a bit of intrigue and adventure," Ruben said, leaning back to check out who was coming through the door.

"I think you're right," I said. "What do you have in mind?"

A broad grin followed a profound silence.

"How about joining me in Amsterdam for a couple of days?"

I hesitated then stopped myself from overanalysing and stressing about the girls. The timing couldn't be more perfect; they're going to the Peak District next week for their silver Duke of Edinburgh hiking and camping award.

"OK, tell me more about this diary you mentioned in your email," I said.

Ruben leaned back in his chair, put his hands behind his head and took a deep breath.

"I mentioned in my email that I recently moved companies and started with an engineering firm in Rotterdam. This company had been supplying steel before and during the war to the Dutch government. It's now one of the largest suppliers of steel in the world. The original owner David Solomon had been in a transit prisoner of war camp called Westerbork during the Second World War. Mr Solomon's nephew, Isaac, has been allocated as my mentor."

"I'm confused. How does a steel company change communication?" I asked, looking at my watch, feeling a bit annoyed at Ruben wasting my time.

"That's just it, my training and induction covered the most thought-provoking module on communication they called 'Communication Intelligence'. I've never come across anything like it before. I believe it's quite pioneering. They state that the reason for their company's success is because of the lessons Mr Solomon learnt during his time in the transit camp—what they called the Fourth Dimension in Communication."

"I've never heard of the Fourth Dimension in Communication," I said. "What does that mean?"

"I'm not sure. All I know is apparently Mr Solomon was part of a group of prisoners who wrote a diary on the secret laws of Communication Intelligence which had at its core the Fourth Dimension in Communication."

"Who were these prisoners? Are they still alive?" I asked, frustrated at the lack of information.

"Isaac didn't know a lot," Ruben said. "He said the prisoners were very well connected before the war, and apparently, one even knew Albert Einstein, but that's about the extent of his knowledge on the diary. I told Isaac I was intrigued to find out more about this diary and asked if he knew of anyone else I could speak to."

"What did he say?" I asked.

"He suggested speaking to a man called Jan Van de Holben, a retired CEO who was very close to Mr Solomon."

"Did you speak to him?" I asked, feeling slightly impatient.

"It took me a while; I finally tracked him down in a nursing home in Rotterdam, only to discover he'd passed away three days earlier," Ruben said.

"You're kidding, so what did you do?"

"To cut a long story short, I managed to speak to Henk, one of Jan's old friends in the nursing home. Henk said Jan had mentioned that a secret diary had been written in the transit camp, but there had been trouble with the Resistance Movement during the war—something to do with a secret society. He couldn't remember much else."

"I don't get it; what's the big deal? Why is it such a secret?" I asked.

"I thought the same thing. I started to dig around on the internet," said Ruben.

"Did you find anything?"

"No, absolutely nothing. I thought it must be a myth or something."

"You have nothing?" I asked, confused as to where this conversation was going.

"Let me finish. I decided to go to the Resistance Movement Museum in Amsterdam to see if anyone there could help. I asked a few guides if they'd ever heard of a secret diary written in Westerbork transit camp that mentioned the Fourth Dimension in Communication."

"Did you find anyone?" I was starting to get a bit bored with the conversation.

"I kept coming across blank faces and total disinterest. As I sat finishing my plate of chips, an older woman sat down at my table and said she'd heard of the secret diary. She looked around cautiously to make sure nobody was within earshot."

"So, what did she say?"

"She said she was a young girl during the war and had also been in the transit camp," Ruben replied. "She said she'd frequently eavesdrop on conversations between important men in the camp. They were very nervous about being caught and would have been shot or put on a train to Auschwitz if they'd been caught collaborating against the Nazis."

I sat up in my seat, becoming increasingly interested in the conversation. "That's incredible. Did the older woman say if she'd seen it?" I asked.

"She said she'd seen a brown leather diary with a key but didn't know what happened to it."

"Did she say if she'd overheard any of the contents of the diary?" I asked.

"As far as she could remember, the diary mentioned the communication strategies used by Hitler during the war to create mass cooperation without resistance. The effects of these strategies were so powerful that the author stressed he believed the diary's contents should not be published until humankind had matured to the extent that they would never repeat the atrocities and total domination subjected by the Nazis."

"I don't get it. Does the diary describe dark psychology?" I asked, but I was not sure I wanted to hear any more.

"I don't think so. She said that the contents of the diary state that when used for good it would create a paradigm shift so large as to completely transform human culture as we know it."

"That's quite a statement," I said, intrigued at the confidence of the writers. "Sorry, who did she say wrote this diary?"

"She said there was a mixture of people from the camp contributing, including a young psychologist who was way ahead of his time and had a very distinguished career after leaving the camp."

"Did she say how many were contributing?"

"She mentioned about five to seven or something. She said that two young men who had contributed had been discovered by German guards hiding in a dark shelter making notes. Their research and writing had not only been destroyed, but they were punished in the most inhumane way. The German guards killed them on the spot in front of their family."

"That's horrendous. Do you know if anyone ever had a copy of the diary or the contents?"

"She said there was a rumour many years ago that a guard in the camp had found it and destroyed it."

"So, it's a wild goose chase then?" I said, sounding disappointed.

Ruben shook his head. "Seems not. As the older woman told me about the diary, she looked down and clasped her hands together, hesitating to go on, unsure whether she could trust me. She cautiously added, 'I heard through a friend of mine that a copy had been made before it was destroyed and divided up. It has five main sections, describing the elements of Communication Intelligence, with the Fourth Dimension in Communication as its core principles. They say the power and effect of the components multiply when used in combination.' "

"Do you believe her?" I asked, still not convinced.

"Like you, I wasn't sure if I believed what she was saying," Ruben replied. "It seemed a bit farfetched, especially in this day and age. My internet searches had not come close to what she'd just revealed." He paused and then continued, "I kept thinking about the timing. They didn't want the diary released until the world was ready."

As I reflected on Ruben's words, I glanced around the café. I immediately witnessed a disturbing argument between a young couple who had spent most of their time looking at their phones rather than engaging in conversation with each other. Without warning, the couple suddenly verbally attacked each other in public, totally oblivious to the attention they attracted. On another table, I saw an older woman sitting alone in front of her laptop, completely transfixed in her digital world. On yet another table, I saw three young people playing on devices but not saying a word to each other. Nobody was aware of anyone else, all engrossed in their own bubble.

"Iris, I think perhaps this is the right time to find the contents of the diary. The world could definitely do with a communication and cultural paradigm shift."

"What else did the woman say?" I asked, returning my attention to Ruben. A waitress appeared, asking if we'd like more drinks and I ordered another coffee.

"Not much else," Ruben answered once the waitress had left. "That's all she knew. She did suggest going to

Westerbork to the transit camp. They have a museum there, and maybe someone else could help."

"OK, so let me get this straight. A secret diary was written in a Dutch transit camp during the Second World War by several prisoners, one of which was a psychologist. It has five sections, and when combined, will create a powerful means of communication, they call Communication Intelligence which will transform relationships and bring about a global cultural shift. Is that right?"

"Yes, I believe so," Ruben replied. "And the reason it was kept secret is because the Dutch government didn't want the contents getting into the wrong hands and being used for evil. The prisoners who wrote it were somehow associated with Mr Solomon, the man who established the business I've just started working for. Somehow the diary outlines the Fourth Dimension in Communication and has connections with Albert Einstein, the Resistance Movement and some sort of secret society."

"Sounds a bit farfetched if you ask me," I said. "You'd think with all the technology in today's world and the current research in neurology, psychology, sociology, behavioural science and behavioural economics, someone would know about these so-called secrets. Are you sure it's not some sort of myth?"

"I thought that too," said Ruben. "But something at the back of my mind kept nagging me to search further. The induction at this new business was like nothing I'd ever experienced before. Mentoring is far superior to any other organisation. Their success is phenomenal; growth has far exceeded every competitor year-on-year since 1945. They've received award after award for excelling at customer service and sales growth. Being a leader in the industry, they take compliance very seriously. Quality assurance, health and safety, environmental compliance are all of the highest standards.

"Interestingly, there is a very diverse range of employees, and integration across multiple generations is seamless. I cannot express how wonderful it is to go to work and see smiles on people's faces. To have enthusiasm and genuine engagement on a daily basis. They must be doing something right. You know, I was thinking, maybe Mr Solomon has the first segment of the diary?"

"Why do you think that?" I asked, wondering where this was going.

"Our induction mentioned the evolution of communication and the importance of Communication Intelligence within the workplace. We began our training by focussing on the Fourth Industrial Revolution. Some call it the Digital Revolution. The company is currently introducing artificial intelligence into practically every department within the organisation. There's a massive training drive on human to machine learning. The company is determined to address all fear surrounding human talent being replaced by machines.

As more people work remotely and replace travel with conference calls, new skills are required. Reading and interpreting nonverbal cues has never been more important. Perhaps if more people learnt about what we're doing, we'll reach a tipping point and transform communication as we know it, maybe even create new social norms?"

"Did anyone at work ever mention the Fourth Dimension in Communication?" I asked.

"Yes, very briefly on our first training day, but it was never mentioned again."

"So, what's your plan?" I asked. It came out sounding more negative than I intended.

"I thought you'd be excited about this. You don't seem convinced," Ruben said.

"I'm a lawyer. I need to see evidence—sorry!" I said, looking at my watch.

"Come to Holland and help me find it. You always did have a knack to see what others couldn't and solve social dilemmas. What happened to the Iris who had endless curiosity and adventure running through her veins?"

"I suppose she grew up, became responsible and forgot how to live and be spontaneous. I'm so serious now, aren't I? I'm not sure I trust people or situations like I used to."

Ruben always did have the ability and awareness to see beyond my façade. He took the time to be present when he was with me. But something had also changed; he seemed to ask more relevant questions and it was like he could read or comprehend beyond our conversation. There was a newfound depth and understanding that I couldn't put my finger on. I felt very safe and at ease, respected maybe. Whatever it was, perhaps it was worth finding out more about Communication Intelligence and the Fourth Dimension in Communication.

"So why has it been so long since we've been in contact?" I asked, changing the subject. "What's happened in the last fifteen years? How are Sarah and the kids, Billy and Jessica isn't it? Are they relocating to Holland with you?" I asked these questions in rapid succession, hardly pausing for breath.

"Sadly not; turns out teenage sweethearts don't always last forever. Sarah and I seem to have grown in different directions," Ruben said.

"I'm so sorry to hear that. What happened?"

"Our hopes and dreams never seemed to land on the same page. She's decided to stay in Sydney with the kids while we trial a six months separation."

"That's really sad," I said. "Do you remember when we were seven years old, and we'd planned our lives together? We spent hours designing our waterfront home, with a jetty."

"Yes, I remember. We had a lot of fun back then in my little rubber dinghy cruising along the river. Our family holidays hold some of my fondest memories. How things have changed," Ruben said, reminiscing. "Perhaps I shouldn't have given my heart away at seven?"

I was about to respond when I spotted a man at another table taking a photo or video of us.

When he noticed I'd seen him, he quickly got up and left. I tried to reach for my phone and take a photo of him, but he was too quick; he'd already disappeared into the crowd.

"Did you see that, Ruben?"

"Yes, weird," he replied, stretching to see who it was. He looked at his watch. "Gosh, look at the time," he added, suddenly getting up. "Must dash, I don't want to be late for my meeting."

Too late, I thought, rolling my eyes.

"Are you coming to Amsterdam?" Ruben said as he ran out the door.

"Why not," I said. "Send me the details."

I felt excited and anxious at the same time. Something I hadn't felt for a very long time. I was still sceptical about the diary and whether there was indeed a new communication framework so powerful it could transform the human race.

It still sounds like a myth. I can understand technology transforming communication such as the radio, telephone or the internet—very two-dimensional understanding. But could there be something more? Could there be a fourth dimension to communication? What are the four dimensions anyway? Wikipedia says it has something to do with time and space and Albert Einstein.

Come to think of it, as a society, we do seem to be disconnected and disengaged. There are far less face-to-face social engagements, a lot more people work remotely, and millennials seem to prefer messaging rather than speaking on the phone or face-to-face. Is the human race ready to make a paradigm shift in communication intelligence? If it's true that there is a secret diary, are we evolved enough to use the knowledge for good rather than evil?

I started replaying the conversation with Ruben in my head. Was the commotion in the psychology department related to the diary? What about the guy who was taking our picture? Was he somehow connected to the university and the missing diary? I wondered if anyone else was looking for the diary. I sat pondering whether it was safe to go to Holland on this search. I didn't want to put my life at risk. I need to be here for my girls; I'm all they have.

I eventually decided there wasn't any harm in spending the weekend in Holland. I'd always loved spending time with Ruben. It couldn't be any more dangerous than coming face to face with snakes and redback spiders in the Australian bush. Could it?

CHAPTER 2

The flight from Heathrow to Amsterdam was smooth but busy. We worked our way through our lengthy agenda, making diligent notes and highlighting areas for further research. I was determined to leave no stone unturned. I would find or crack the communication code one way or another in the shortest time possible. I had a new mission and felt alive.

Ruben gently brought me back down to earth just as the plane was landing. Our first stop was brunch with Mr Solomon's nephew, Isaac, who was Ruben's mentor.

"Listen, Iris, no cross-examining Isaac; he's not in the witness box, and this isn't the Spanish inquisition. Be gentle. Let me lead," Ruben said, gathering all his belongings.

Fine, I thought, but I'm sure I'll have to jump in and rescue the situation.

The scepticism started creeping back. How on earth are we supposed to find five missing sections of a secret diary written seventy-six years ago by unknown authors in a prisoner of war transit camp? Is this just a waste of time and a wild goose chase? I don't have the time or energy to go digging round in mouldy boxes and muddy trenches. But I suppose it does break the humdrum of my usual papers in, papers out daily routine. Luckily, Ruben and I had grown up in Dutch households. Both our parents migrated to Australia shortly after the Second World War. Our parents met through the Dutch community. We went to the same Dutch butcher, same Dutch baker, and had the same crazy Dutch carpet on our tables. Growing up in a bilingual home would finally have a benefit.

o o o

Isaac was the most helpful man. He had an air and presence about him that was beyond anything I'd ever encountered before. I'd done a quick Google search on him before we met. He was a leading authority in communication and a keynote speaker at industry events, having published many thought-provoking articles in industry publications on communication. His web shadow was impeccable. He was exceptionally well presented in the most ordinary way. Confident, yet deeply respectful. The pure definition of calm, authentic and honourable.

After our pleasant introductions, I decided to stop wasting time, jumped straight in, and asked him to describe his communication strategy's essence.

Without missing a beat, he followed my lead and got right to the point.

He said, "My uncle Mr Solomon had often quoted his friend Viktor Frankl in their company inductions and training. Solomon Steel trainers lead by stating this quote: *'We identify more with that of an eye specialist than a painter. A painter tries to convey to us a picture of the world as he sees it. An ophthalmologist tries to enable us to see the world as it really is.'* "

Isaac paused and then went on to explain: "The framework behind our Communication Model is to enhance our employee's Communication Intelligence. To shine a light on the whole spectrum of possible meaning received from every form of communication, whether verbal or nonverbal."

"Gosh, that's profound. I'm a bit confused," I said. "Where do you start?"

"It's essential and helps to understand the historical evolution of communication," Isaac continued. "Revolutions don't only bring about technological change but changes in communication, thoughts and feelings. We're currently in the Fourth Industrial Revolution—a continuation of the Third Industrial Revolution—also known as the Digital Revolution, that commenced in the middle of the last century around the Second World War. The digital revolution impacts not only business but also our personal lives. In recent years we've seen a significant shift in utilising online platforms to book flights, make payments, obtain the latest news and updates, listen to music, watch TV and movies, to name just a few. The level and velocity of disruption to all industries due to this communication revolution is unprecedented. Enhanced consumer engagement and expectations, along with global platforms, are forcing companies to re-examine their business and communication models almost daily. There has never been a better time to change traditional, linear thinking and communication to effectively manage the magnitude of disruption and innovation currently shaping our future."

"Sorry, could you translate that into English, please?" I asked, somewhat confused.

"In a nutshell, humans need to accept they cannot compete with machines, robotics and artificial intelligence. They do not have the memory capacity, speed or analytical skills to outperform a machine. Humans should focus on their unique communication abilities, their empathy, creativity, humour and kindness. If humankind were to focus on upscaling these skills, we'd shortly reach a tipping point and move our moral compass to a shared sense of collaboration, acceptance and cultural awareness."

"OK, that makes a lot more sense," I said, grateful for the clarification. "How do we upscale our skills though?"

"What we need to understand is communication is on the listener's terms. Listeners comprehend purely through their frames of reference, biases and preconceived ideas," Isaac explained slowly. "When most people communicate, they only think about the message they are verbally sharing. They're not generally aware of the listener's needs. A listener's mind is a moving target, constantly oscillating between his or her own thoughts and the speaker's ongoing message. Ironically everyone is conscious that they tune in and out of conversations, but believe their listener remains constantly attuned to their message."

"Interesting, I'd never thought about communicating like that. What do you mean by aware?" I asked, reconsidering the doubts I'd been having.

"Up until recently, most organisations utilised a hierarchical structure. They had non-negotiable operating systems, procedural manuals, policies and procedures. Most employees were employed to follow instructions and create consistent outcomes; they were not employed to be creative, innovative or design new ways of thinking," Isaac said.

"Yes, I can vouch for that," Ruben said, remembering why he left his last job. "My last boss was a total dictator, from the old school of 'Do as I say, not as I do.' "

"Exactly," Isaac concurred.

"Until recently, most of the workforce felt trapped in a pattern of emotional slavery. At work and home, there was a feeling of constantly striving to keep everyone happy. Feeling overwhelmed, stressed and responsible for the feelings and wellbeing of others. Guilt and fear ran through the veins pushing personal needs to the background."

"I can relate to that," I said, "but I don't believe my girls will put up with the same authoritarian behaviour."

"Very interesting point, Iris," Isaac said. "Millennials have benefited from being the most educated generation in history. They're more independent and have shifted humankind to an obnoxious stage. In general, they are more aware of themselves, stating, 'That's not my problem,' or 'I'm not responsible for your feelings.' In most cases, millennials are better at expressing their needs and more comfortable at dealing with others' displeasure. We are currently in a crucial stage in our development and personal growth, leading us directly into the emotional liberation stage."

"What is emotional liberation?" Ruben asked.

"Emotional liberation means feeling liberated not to take on the feelings, stresses and concerns of others," Isaac explained. "Awareness in communication allows us to respond to others' needs out of compassion, not guilt, shame or fear. Awareness allows us to take full responsibility for our intentions and actions but not others' feelings and actions. A sense of freedom and liberation combined with confidence and trust envelope? emotionally liberated communication skills. In other words, having Communication Intelligence."

"Can you tell me what I need to do to increase my awareness and create emotional liberation?" I asked.

"An excellent question, Iris. Communication is not only about verbal communication. Nonverbal cues are approximately 70% of communication. Most people don't realise, nonverbal communication is not only body language but the image you project, the clothes you wear, the car you drive, the state of your workspace. Your reputation does precede you. Most people don't fully appreciate the impact of their web shadow. Most people will do a web search before meeting someone new."

I went a shade of crimson and looked down.

"People will make all sorts of judgements based on your qualifications, social media content and your circle of friends. Time and place are also fundamental cues. Are you known for being on time, organised, reliable and polite? Do you know what silent messages you're sending out?" Isaac asked.

"I'd never thought about that," I said. "I'm usually only concerned about getting my message across. I don't even check to see if the person fully understood what I said." I was somewhat embarrassed by my confession. "Isaac, I know this is a bit bold," I added, "but do you know if there are any notes used to refer to your communication training modules? Maybe Mr Solomon left behind some notes he made during the war?"

"Come to think of it; there are," he replied. "We have an archive warehouse in Rotterdam. I was there only the other day looking at some old records from just after the war. I'd asked a colleague to go through and see if there was anything not relevant we could destroy, as we're rapidly running out of space. I can't make any promises, but I'm happy to drive you to the warehouse and see if we can locate the old notes."

o o o

The warehouse was simply spectacular, with the most advanced configuration I'd ever seen. Even Amazon would be impressed. I can honestly say it brought organisation to a whole new level. Isaac took us to the 1920-1945 section from establishment to post-war. He gave us some very old boxes labelled 1942-1945 and said this was the time frame Mr Solomon had mentioned he was in the prisoner of war transit camp.

The boxes were very fragile and held a lot of invoices and financial documents. We spent a good five hours in the warehouse and were about to give up, when Isaac remembered Mr Solomon's personal box. Hoping and silently praying it hadn't been shredded, I noticed the colour suddenly drain from Isaac's face; his eyebrows went down, revealing a sombre look. I felt goosebumps rush down my spine and instant panic. Had he found what he was looking for, or were all our hopes dashed and the missing section lost forever?

Isaac was looking inside Mr Solomon's cardboard box, which was empty.

"What's wrong?" I asked. "You look like you've seen a ghost."

"I've never seen this false bottom before," Isaac said, lifting a flap.

We all looked inside the box and saw an old silver tin, slightly rusty and dented but on the whole in remarkable condition. Isaac carefully opened the lid. It was like entering an Aladdin's cave. A waft of old tobacco and musk filled the air. It felt like we were instantly transported back to the transit camp. Inside the box, we found Mr Solomon's prisoner of war ID card, his yellow Star of David armband, a food coupon and an empty Camel Cigarette packet with $CI = (AO + EU) \times I$ written on it. At the very bottom was what looked like a section of a diary. Two pages of notes with drawings, some words on a page that looked like it was a code to something and a set of keys. We couldn't believe our luck. Grinning and shaking with excitement, I asked Isaac if it would be OK to take a photo of the notes and packet of cigarettes. A long silence followed as Isaac carefully examined the contents of the tin and notes. After what seemed like forever, he allowed me to take photos of the two pages, the page with code and the packet of cigarettes. Ever so grateful, I thanked him profusely, then very boldly asked if it would be OK if we borrowed the old set of keys.

Isaac smiled, paused, took a closer look at the set of keys and then said, "It would be my honour and pleasure to help you find what you are looking for. The keys don't seem to relate to anything in the business so it should be fine."

As I was reading the notes found in the tin, it felt like I was struck by lightning. I opened my mouth but not a single word came out.

"What is it?" asked Ruben. "You're never lost for words."

I handed him the piece of paper and let him read for himself:

Communication Intelligence—The Philosophy

Communication Intelligence is an integrated philosophy of real life and conscious understanding.

The heart of this philosophy seeks to rehumanise communication to embrace the whole-mind, whole-body and whole-system to create a wholly unique interactive experience. As such it aims to replace many of the limiting beliefs, values, and practices from the past.

It focusses on collaboration and interconnectedness. It sets the scene for a communication rich environment appealing to all personality types, being all-inclusive.

Intelligence

We use the term intelligence regarding Communication Intelligence in the way humans think, comprehend, reason and integrate images and experiences.

Communication Intelligence connects the mind, body, emotions, environment, and intuitive experience to bring a wholistic meaning to communication.

The Aim of Communication Intelligence

The aim of Communication Intelligence is to awaken communicators to their full potential, to make communicating enjoyable and fulfilling. To master skills in the Laws of Human Relations. To gain confidence, enhance engagement, improve status, impact, and influence.

Communication Intelligence aims to contribute to human intelligence, competence, happiness and ultimate success.

The Fourth Dimension in Communication

Examines human activities through time and space. Territorial behaviour which defines a unit of space depends on the frame of reference a person employs. Intellectual observations in communication will depend on points of view, timeframes, and astuteness of the observer.

Time is a commodity. We earn it, spend it, and frequently waste it. It's a non-renewable resource that impacts every form of communication.

1. Awareness—The first principle in Communication Intelligence

We take inspiration from Albert Einstein:

"Once man's psychological impediments are resolved the real problems in society won't be such a difficult matter. In the past it was enough for a man to free himself of his personal egotism to make him valuable to society, today he must also overcome national and class egotism and bias. Only when he relieves these burdens can he contribute toward improving the lot of humanity and his ability to communicate."

"Can I see that?" Isaac said as he stretched out his arm. "It sounds very familiar. I believe we use it in our communication training."

"I remember," Ruben said. "It was part of our Awareness module."

"Yes, that's it," Isaac confirmed. "We begin our induction training with everyone becoming aware of themselves, their beliefs and values, their priorities and exercises to explore unconscious bias."

Suddenly curious, I asked Isaac, "Has anyone else ever asked to see more details about your communication modules and the Fourth Dimension in Communication?"

"Interestingly, yes," Isaac reminisced. "We had a very talented young apprentice called Bogdan Kosov a couple of years ago. He seemed fascinated by our training modules and asked the most intelligent well thought out questions. He left us about eighteen months ago to pursue his career in fabrication. I believe he moved to Germany."

Isaac graciously asked if we'd like a coffee before heading back to Amsterdam. Looking at his watch, he mentioned he had other matters to attend to in an hour.

While Isaac got fresh coffee, I looked Bogdan up on LinkedIn. I discovered he's working for Hans Bokman, in a fabrication company in Birmingham. He's completing a Masters in Behavioural Science and Interventions at Oxford University.

Wait a minute. He looks familiar; he looks just like the man taking photos of us in the coffee house in Oxford on Thursday. Could it be the same man?

CHAPTER 3

"How was dinner with your cousin?" Ruben asked while we stood in line, waiting for our coffee and pancakes.

"Good, she still doesn't stop talking. I've never come across anyone who talks as fast or as much as her. Sorry I couldn't make dinner. I felt obliged as I haven't seen her in years. It was quite interesting, though; I explained to her why I was here and about searching for the diary. She suddenly got out some old photo albums from her parents. Remember how I told you our grandfathers were brothers? Well, she reminded me how they didn't see eye to eye because, during the war, her grandfather was a naval officer, and my grandfather, who was also in the navy, was transferred to a transit camp."

"Do you know which one?" Ruben asked, sitting up straight.

"Unfortunately, not. My grandparents never really spoke about the war. They were so sweet and lovely. Whenever I saw them, they'd asked lots of questions about school, then work and listened intently to my stories. When I was a teenager, I remember they were in the paper and on TV, but I'm ashamed to say I don't know a lot about it. I think they got a medal of righteousness or something, and a tree was planted in their honour in Israel for saving Jews during the war. I was a typical teenager back then, totally absorbed in my daily dramas. The war seemed like the olden days and so far removed from my life."

"Would you like vanilla in your coffee?" the waitress asked. "A table has just become available overlooking the canal. Would that be OK?"

"Yes, thanks," I replied. Turning to Ruben, I asked, "How was your evening?"

"Very interesting," Ruben replied. "I spent the night researching Westerbork Transit Camp and the photos of the notes from Mr Solomon's tin box. Google maps came up with lots of interesting facts and images of the transit camp."

"So, what do you think we should do next?" I asked. "Do you have a plan?"

"Yes, I think we should make our way to Westerbork after breakfast. They're only open until 4 p.m. today. Mr Solomon's notes included a map of the site with some names on it. Let's see what we can find. I can drive; it should only take about forty minutes."

"Where is it compared to Amsterdam?" I asked.

"It's in a very remote part of Drenthe in the north-eastern region. I'll take you the scenic way so you can see the quaint houses on the canal in an area known as the Little Venice of Holland. If we have time, we can take a boat ride along the canals and pop in for pizza before heading back."

o   o   o

As we pulled up to Westerbork, I noticed only a few cars in the visitor car park. It looked like we'd stepped back into 1942. We were surrounded by people of all ages, happily cycling along designated cycle lanes. There were a significant number of people on the road for a quiet country town, either cycling with shopping, couples cycling deep in conversation expertly negotiating the crowd and parents with babies strapped in seats attached to the front handlebars of their bike. I was mesmerised by the calm and tranquillity of it all.

"Come on, Iris, there's not much time, get with the programme," Ruben said. "You'll have plenty of time later to take in the sights."

The museum was immaculate. It was immediately apparent that the curators had spent hours ensuring the inmates' dignity and sensitivity to privacy. They found the right balance of photos, historical artefacts and images of life in the camp. We took our time reading an assortment of personal stories and tried to find any clues that might indicate the writing of a secret diary. I was amazed to find out Anne Frank and her family had come through the transit camp before being sent to Auschwitz. I asked the woman at reception if it was possible to go inside the camp. A very firm "no" was her reply.

"Everything you need to see is here," she said. Then she went straight back to her computer. Conversation closed!

Ruben and I decided to go back outside and walk along the old train track that transported prisoners to other prisoner of war camps. We noticed an older man with a vintage wooden rake, stooped over sweeping some leaves. "Hello," I said, "do you speak English?"

"Yes," he said.

"I was wondering if you could give us a bit more information," Ruben said. "Do you know much about the history of Westerbork?"

The old man smiled broadly, "Yes, I do," he said. "What do you want to know?"

"How long have you worked here?" Ruben asked.

"I no longer work here; I simply volunteer and keep to myself," the man replied matter-of-factly.

"Did you work here during the war?" Ruben asked politely.

"When I was a very young man, my first job after leaving school was as a civil servant working in the Justice Department in the Central Food Distribution Office in the Hague. When the war broke out, I was transferred to Camp Westerbork to help with food distribution for the prisoners of war."

"My grandparents also worked in a transit camp," I said. "Did you ever hear of Janus and Willemina De Jong?"

The older man looked at me astounded, then fell silent, a tear rolled down his cheek.

"My child," he said. "Janus was my boss, and Willemina was a very good friend of my wife. Such a young couple when they arrived in 1941 with their small child Johanna. They were so brave, constantly risking their own lives to stop people going on the trains to Theresienstadt ghetto, Bergen-Belsen and Auschwitz concentration camps."

I felt a shiver run down my spine. "Johanna is my mother," I said in shock.

"How are they?" he asked.

"Sadly, my grandmother passed away more than twenty years ago from cancer, and my grandfather passed away seven years ago," I said. "I miss them terribly. My parents lived in Australia, however, they both also passed away a few years ago." I felt myself becoming emotional, so tried to compose myself. "Would you mind telling me a bit more about my grandparents?" I asked. "I'm embarrassed to say I don't know a lot about what happened here."

"I'd be delighted," the old man said. "It would do me the greatest honour to fill in the gaps; it's the least I can do for all they did to help others here. As you know, your grandparents were Christians, not Jews. They, like me, had been transferred here and knew nothing about the true extent of the Nazis and their propaganda. Westerbork was unique in as far that it was not a ghetto or concentration camp. It was a transit camp."

"What was the difference between a concentration camp and a transit camp?" I asked.

"A transit camp held prisoners for a short period of time before deportation to other Nazi camps. There were many different types of concentration camps throughout Europe with forced labour and extermination facilities."

"You mentioned that my grandparents stopped many people going on trains to other camps. How did they do that?" I asked. I was fascinated by his depth of knowledge.

"Your grandfather held an administration position within Camp Westerbork and could employ people as essential workers to distribute food, clean, and help with office administration. He was also the registration clerk, which meant everyone who came through the camp had to be fingerprinted and registered. Luckily back then, there were no computers, so it was easy for identification cards to simply go missing, meaning there was no trace of that prisoner ever being registered in the camp."

"That sounds very dangerous, tampering with registration cards," I said. "Who was in charge of the camp?"

"The Germans had invaded Holland, resulting in the camp being run by Germans with some Dutch personnel in administrative positions, which included your grandparents and me."

"It must have been tough to decide whom to help and which lives to save," I said, feeling deep sorrow for my grandparents.

"Your grandparents weren't concerned about the colour of people's skin, nor what their beliefs or values were. If someone needed help, they would do whatever they could to help save a life. Many of us did the same with our small amount of power. Not everyone was kind, however. The camp commander and the guards were very strict and could be exceptionally violent. We learnt very quickly whom we could trust and created many codes and symbols as an alternative form of communication. We also had many suppliers who helped people escape. The local farmers who supplied our fresh produce came weekly in their delivery vans. Most of them were also part of the Resistance Movement. We managed to smuggle several prisoners out in their vans."

"Did you ever hear of a secret diary on Communication Intelligence or the Fourth Dimension in Communication?" I asked.

"Yes, my dear, I did." At the old man's words, I felt goosebumps all over. "My name is Jorgen Jensen, by the way."

Jorgen motioned for us to follow him, so we did so. "Come with me," he said. "I'll take you within the camp. But stay close to me. The administrators refuse to allow any outsiders to come within the wired fence. There are CCTV cameras everywhere. If anyone approaches, go down the side lane next to the big house that used to be the Commanders house. Your grandparent's house used to be next door to the big house. After the war, they demolished almost the entire camp. You'll find an old barn just past the big house. Keep going past the barn, to the left of the third tree, you'll find a trapdoor. Make your way over there. There's no CCTV."

When we finally walked inside the camp, there was a deathly silence. Only a few large trees and a vast field remained. Every speck of evidence of the war and the inhumane treatment of inmates had been annihilated. I felt a surge of annoyance rapidly rising.

"Jorgen, why have they removed all evidence of the war and suffering?" I asked, trying to keep my rage at a lower simmer.

"Many have asked the same question. Many have felt as strongly as you do. All I can say is this: 'Take someone who doesn't keep score, who's not looking to be richer, or afraid of losing, who has not the slightest interest even in his own personality: He is truly free.'—Rumi."

As we continued walking among the trees, Jorgen added, "During the war, both the Dutch government and Dutch royal family were in exile in London. People from all backgrounds were trying to break the psychological stronghold Hitler held over the people and prevent further psychological warfare. Secret societies were formed with the most brilliant intellectuals from all parts of the world, including Albert Einstein. These secret societies were committed to try and combat the atrocities inflicted all over the world. Nobody was ever sure whom to trust. The society for intellectuals and cooperation was one such society. It was non-political with a manifesto to include intellectuals of all nations isolated by war to communicate with each other and share ideas."

"Was there a secret society within the camp?" Ruben asked. I could see that he too was captivated by the extent of Jorgen's knowledge.

"Those within the camp and directly involved in the day to day running of the camp created an underground movement. Underground meetings and escape plans were high voltage requiring extreme secrecy and caution with dire consequences not only to the perpetrator of illegal activities but also for the family of those who had escaped the camp. If a family member was discovered to have escaped, it resulted in immediate execution or transportation to an unknown destination of no return for the remaining family members. We lived by the rule of—imminent threat of death sharpens a man's wits."

"Were you part of a secret society or underground movement?" Ruben asked.

"No, I wasn't a member of a secret society; I was a member of the Resistance Movement, which was an underground movement," Jorgen explained. "We had members in the Resistance Movement who were members of various secret societies though, and they would openly share their knowledge."

"What happened at Resistance Movement meetings?" I asked.

"We had members both within the camp and outside the camp, trying to help prisoners escape. We would discuss the guards' movements, who was making deliveries into the camp, who was willing to help, who had what power within the camp and what dangers we faced."

"You must have had a large pool of diverse people within the camp who had experience in an extraordinary number of mixed occupations," I said.

"Indeed we did," Jorgen confirmed. "We were able to draw on the wisdom of a phenomenal amount of men and women in the camp, who were very well respected in their field, such as psychology, before the war."

"I think we still have a lot to learn from a psychological perspective from the Second World War," I said, feeling deflated by all the suffering.

"It's most unfortunate, Camp Westerbork and the extermination camps should never have happened," Jorgen said. "It resulted from failed world politics and a society driven by the suggestive influence of the psychological superiority in Germany. Hitler and his officers inflicted a radicalisation process never before seen in the history of humanity. Outside of the camp, people were indifferent to and silent towards the suffering within."

"Did everyone registered in the camp end up being transported to another camp?" I asked.

"Not everyone but nearly everyone sent to Westerbork, around 100,000 people were eventually transported by train to an unknown destination in Eastern Europe, later known as Sobibor, Auschwitz and other death camps in Poland."

"Did the prisoners get much warning when they would leave?" Ruben enquired.

"No, people were in a constant state of heightened anxiety, fear and crisis. Prisoners never knew from one day to the next if their name would appear on the deportation train list. People had an overwhelming feeling of powerless and deep sorrow." I could see the sadness in Jorgen's eyes as he relived the pain.

We were just under the Watch Tower when a deafening siren suddenly went off. Ruben and I jumped and shot each other a petrified look. We saw some guards yell at us, waving a gun.

"Quick, go to the trapdoor and make your way to Roland Boerman; tell him I sent you," said Jorgen.

We ran like we've never run before. We heard shots in the air and I was too scared to look back. I don't know where I got the strength or stamina, but something pushed me to keep going. We ran towards the Commander's house, then down the lane. Where was that trapdoor, second or third tree? Oh my god, I can't remember. I followed Ruben, desperately searching in the long grass for the wooden door. I couldn't think straight; I was so scared and could only think of my girls and how stupid I was to search for the diary. "Found it!" said Ruben. "But it's jammed! The grass has grown over half the door." After a mad scramble, we removed the dirt and opened the door. We jumped in, turned on the torches on our phones and legged it for all we were worth. Panting desperately, I struggled to keep going. However, there was just no way I could stop. Finally, we saw another wooden door. I hesitated.

"Wait," I said, "don't open the door. What if the guards are waiting for us on the other side?"

"I don't think they could get to us that quickly," Ruben said. "We've gone under a field. They'd have to get in their car and drive about seven miles to get to us."

"Good point," I said, "but let's open the hatch ever so slightly, take a photo with our phone and see if it's safe."

I opened the hatch and moved my phone so the camera was positioned in the small opening. I looked at the photo; it showed an image of a very derelict, abandoned barn. Once satisfied that no one was waiting for us, Ruben and I cautiously but quickly left the tunnel and stepped inside. To our relief, we found a couple of hay bales, some crates, some old blankets and a couple of old black bikes with lots of cobwebs; luckily the tyres weren't flat. Hiding behind the hay bales, we decided to regroup and figure out our next move.

"Look at this", Ruben said as he showed me the map from Mr Solomon's tin box. "This must be the barn with the big tree and electrical pole. The map shows there's a farmhouse just down the path.

Let's take the bikes and join a crowd of cyclists," Ruben continued, "that way, we can blend in, just in case someone from the museum or the police come looking for us."

We cycled for about fifteen minutes on a flat road inhaling the strong smell of cows. The leafless trees on each side of the road felt quite eerie, like arms coming out to get us as the fog began rolling in, and the rain gently fell upon us. The twilight evening did, however, make it more difficult to spot us on the run.

Approaching a traditional brown wooden farmhouse with a peaked roof and green painted window shutters, I felt elation and fear simultaneously. What on earth were we getting ourselves into?

This is madness, I thought. I'm a mother, I'm a professional, I must be going out of my mind, chasing a myth about a secret diary.

Just at that moment, a motion sensor light came on, and two big black hairy dogs started barking and coming towards us. "Oh great, just what we need," I said.

"Don't panic," said Ruben as a short, stocky man came out. "Willem, Alexander sit!" the stocky man said to the dogs.

"Can I help you?" the man asked in Dutch.

"I hope so," said Ruben. "Do you speak English?"

"Yes, a little," he said in perfect English.

"Good, we were just at the Westerbork Museum speaking to Mr Jansen," Ruben said. "As we were led around the camp by Mr Jensen, some guards got angry. Mr Jansen suggested going through the underground tunnel and make our way to Roland Boerman. He said Mr Boerman might be able to help us. Do you happen to know someone by that name?"

"That brings back memories," the stocky man said. He gestured for us to come into the house. "Come in," he said. "I do know someone by that name. My name is Roland—Roland Boerman."

After several cups of tea and the most delicious plate of traditional Dutch cheese, we explained the whole story going back to Mr Solomon, the secret diary and the tin we'd found in the archive box. Roland remained primarily silent throughout the entire conversation, smiling. He finally spoke, saying, "That's quite an adventure you two have had. Tell me, what do you think about all of this?"

"I think we're out of our depth and need help," I confessed.

Just then, a woman walked into the kitchen.

"Hello," Ruben and I said.

"This is my wife, Gerda," said Roland. "She's deaf, but she can lipread, and she's proficient in sign language. Can you sign?"

"I can," I said very happily. I recently went on a professional development course on sign language for my diversity and inclusion compulsory training.

"I'm impressed," said Ruben.

"It's the most awesome skill to have. It opens up a whole new world. To be able to communicate with someone through sign is beyond words," I said eagerly.

"Clearly," said Ruben.

Gerda and I conversed for a bit, before I turned back to Roland and asked, "Did you know my grandparents Janus and Willemina De Jong?"

"Indeed I did," he said. "I was just a young boy of ten when the war started. I used to help my parents around the farm, with work and with the many people who came to our farm with desperation in their eyes. I remember your grandmother very well; she had kind eyes. You have her eyes and the same smile."

I smiled back proudly and remembered sitting on my grandmother's lap as a child. She would often say: *"Whatever lifts the corner of your mouth, trust that."*

"Why did my grandmother come here?" I asked.

"Your grandmother would cycle over here once a week with papers. She worked as a courier for the Resistance Movement," Roland explained. "She always looked so pretty and even had a baby during her time at Westerbork; nobody suspected her of carrying papers. Another member of the Resistance Movement, Mr Slager, our neighbour down the road, brought meat and eggs into the camp every week; he concealed escapees in the back of his van behind crates and animal carcasses. He would deliver these people to other resistance workers such as us. We would then help them move further away into the cities. We were able to do this by giving the escapees forged documents, including false baptismal certificates, which made it possible for prisoners to claim they weren't Jews so as not to be deported. We used to hide people in our little room out the back. Would you like to see it?"

"Yes, please!" Ruben and I said in unison.

Roland got up and led us into a tiny dark room. The only furniture was a table which he pushed aside, as well as the carpet beneath, to reveal a small door that led to a bunker.

"Come inside, and I'll show you around," Roland said. "We hid many men, women and children in this room."

We descended a small ladder into a bunker. It looked like the room hadn't been touched since 1945. It still had old metal plates and cups in the cupboard. On the far shelf were books and an old newspaper dated 12th April 1945— the day Holland was liberated.

I noticed a wooden box on the shelf. "What's in the box?" I asked curiously.

"Excellent question, my dear. Some old papers, I think. It belonged to my father. We can't find the key, and I don't have the heart to break it."

"Did you ever hear of the Fourth Dimension in Communication or the term Communication Intelligence?" I asked.

"I overheard many things when I hid during Resistance Movement meetings. The Fourth Dimension in Communication does sound familiar, but I don't know a lot about it. My brother Kurt, however, was fascinated by it."

"Would it be possible to speak to him?" I asked, trying to suppress my excitement.

"I can't see why not. Kurt is a very busy man, however. He lives in Belgium and runs a hugely successful logistics and transport business. I'll give him a call and see if he's available."

While Roland left the bunker and went to speak to his brother, I whispered to Ruben, "Did you bring the set of keys from Mr Solomon's tin box? Let's see if one fits in the box on the shelf."

"I don't think so! I ran out the door in a hurry, not wanting to be late again! Sorry!"

CHAPTER 4

"What?" I asked, surprised, giving him the filthiest look. "What do you mean, you don't have the keys? You had one job—one job!"

"Hang on a minute," Ruben said, looking at me quizzically. "Didn't I give you the keys? Remember last night when we squabbled about how I always lost my blue Rip Curl wallet, with the Velcro strap that didn't stick, along with my house key? I tossed the keys to you. I think you threw them in your handbag—you said you'd put them in a safe place."

I suddenly remembered and felt like an idiot. "Oh yeah, that's right. Sorry. I was so taken by the new bag that I'd gotten for Christmas with pockets within pockets. I forgot about the keys."

I quickly scrambled through my bag, looking for the keys but couldn't find them. I took everything out and still nothing. "Weird, I'm sure they must be in here," I muttered, confused and flustered.

"Look again," Ruben said quickly.

"I am," I said whilst looking at the entire contents of my handbag on the table. "It doesn't make sense. Someone must have stolen them," I concluded.

After several minutes of desperate searching, I stopped.

"Oh, that's right, I attached them to my house keys so I wouldn't lose them. Here they are," I suddenly said, smiling broadly.

Ruben grabbed the keys and went to find Roland who said it was fine to try the keys in his wooden box.

Ruben returned and we began to test the keys. With each one we inserted, we waited with bated breath to see if it would work. The first fit but wouldn't turn, the second was the complete wrong shape, and the third fit the lock. Roland slowly turned the key and opened the box. Again, we smelt the same strong smell of tobacco.

Roland carefully started going through the contents. He found old identity cards, distribution cards, forged identity papers, lots of paper in different sizes with old letterhead from Westerbork, a rubber stamp with the commander of the camp's signature and one from the Commander-in-Chief of the Occupied Netherland Territories. It looked like all the tools and resources used by the Resistance Movement. As we kept searching, we found a separate envelope with the same handwriting as the notes we found in Mr Solomon's tin box. Inside were three pages describing the second principle in Communication Intelligence.

Ruben read:

2. Empathy—The second principle in Communication Intelligence.

We take inspiration from Aristotle, who was the first to design a communication model.

A speaker must be very careful about his selection of words and content in this model of communication. He should understand his target audience and then prepare his speech. The politician must understand the needs of the people in his constituency, then design his speech. It's not what you say; it's what people hear. Empathy is the key.

You may compose the most succinct message in the world. However, it will still be received and understood through the prism of the receiver's own emotions, pre-conceptions, prejudices and pre-existing beliefs and experiences.

Ruben and I could not believe our luck. We'd found the second principle so quickly.

"Roland, would it be OK to take some photos of these notes?" Ruben asked. Roland had joined us in the bunker to see if we had indeed discovered the key to the old box.

"Yes, of course. My brother Kurt also confirmed noon tomorrow would be convenient to have a meeting. Here are his details in Brussels." He handed me a card. "Would you like me to drive you back to your car?" Roland said. "It's getting late, and I still have some jobs to do around the farm."

"Thanks, Roland," Ruben said, "but what about the bikes?"

"Don't worry about them; I'll have one of the boys take them back in the morning," he said.

o o o

By the time we got back to the museum, it was pitch black. Only Rubens's car was left in the car park.

"Thank goodness, I was anxious someone would be waiting for us," I said.

We drove in silence for quite a while. I was deep in thought, going over everything that had happened since we arrived. Meeting Isaac and learning about Mr Solomon and the transit camp, finding the tin box, learning about the evolution and importance of awareness in communication—discovering more about my grandparents from Mr Jansen and their part in the transit camp. Meeting Roland and his lovely wife Gerda, how warm and welcoming they were. Showing us their bunker and learning about the risks people took during the war to help unknown members of the community.

Suddenly, out of the corner of my eye, I noticed a blue light coming closer towards us and then a siren.

"You have *got* to be kidding," I hissed to Ruben. "Were you speeding?"

"No."

"Oh, really?"

"Honestly, I wasn't," he insisted as he pulled the car over.

Just then, a very tall, slim police officer with a bullet-proof vest and gun attached to his belt knocked on the window and asked to see Ruben's driver's licence.

"Can you get it out of my wallet, babe, it's in your handbag, just behind my Albert Hein card," Ruben said.

"What's the problem, officer? What has he done? What's going on?" I asked, desperately trying to work out why we were stopped.

"Please ask your wife to remain quiet," the police officer said.

Slow down, I thought. I am not his wife. I am not anyone's wife.

It'd been a very long time since someone called me a wife. The nerve of some people to jump to conclusions.

I decided, at this point, it was probably best to keep my opinions to myself.

"The reason we stopped your vehicle is that the Westerbork Museum notified us that you had trespassed on their property. Your number plate was picked up by our street cameras and sent through to our database," the officer explained. "We spoke to a volunteer at the museum who confirmed he had invited you onto the museum land. However, you did not stop when the alarm went off. As there was no damage to the property, I'm prepared to let you both off with a warning. However, I must also let you know your right brake light isn't working."

"Thank you, officer," Ruben said.

"I just noticed, the car management system warning light has come on as well. I'm heading straight home to

Rotterdam. I'll have my mechanic look at it in the morning," Ruben confirmed.

With that, the police officer returned to his car.

"Oh my god, can you believe it? How dare he? We didn't do anything wrong! What an arrogant…"

"Settle down, Iris, it's going to be OK. He did have a point," Ruben said calmly.

I took a deep breath and felt seriously unimpressed. My mind was overflowing with doubt, and my enthusiasm was rapidly fading. I admit, Isaac made some valid points, but at the same time, I felt no desire to get any further involved in this mythological wartime discovery tour.

I thought about how this wasn't my problem. How it had nothing to do with me.

Why should I risk my life and reputation? I thought. Would we be able to make a difference to the world even if we did find all the missing parts to the secret diary? I was about to tell Ruben to hang a left and drop me at the airport. Then, I thought about my grandparents, how they had been so brave at only twenty-three years old when they first entered the camp. They had a lot more to lose, and were in a lot more danger than me. They spent four years living in fear, with death all around them. I suddenly felt ashamed. I would be a coward to give up now. With a new sense of determination running through my veins, I decided I wouldn't turn a blind eye to the unnecessary suffering during the war. I would make my grandparents proud. I resolved to find the missing parts of the lost diary.

"You know what I think, Rissy?" Ruben said, breaking my thoughts. The sound of his pet-name for me made me smile. "We should find a warm, cosy restaurant and have a bite to eat. There's a great little restaurant around the corner from mine with a wonderful wine bar, open fire and the best Italian in town. We can regroup and make a plan for tomorrow."

"Sounds good to me," I said.

The restaurant was divine, with classic wooden tables, green décor and black and white photos of Hollywood stars like Audrey Hepburn in *Roman Holiday*, a car scene from the *Italian Job*, photos of Cary Grant, Sean Connery, Elizabeth Taylor, Sophia Loren and Frank Sinatra.

Dinner went by in the blink of an eye. It had been a very long time since I'd had such a wonderful evening. The ambience, sensational food, excellent choice of wine and the most delicious dessert certainly helped. We laughed like in the old days and came up with a plan for tomorrow.

We arranged to meet at 9:45 am the following day at Centraal Station in Rotterdam. Ruben had a bit of work to do and a conference call with Isaac at 8:30 a.m. We decided to catch the 10 a.m. train to Brussels, as his car needed a service. The train would only take an hour and a half, which gave us plenty of time to catch a taxi to Kurt's office to be there at noon.

CHAPTER 5

MONDAY, 10 A.M.

I 'd waited and waited until 9:55 a.m. but had to get on the train. Where was Ruben? I'd just gotten off the phone with the girls, and my battery was dead. Oh well, I'll see him on the train. With a bit of luck, I can charge my phone on the train, I thought.

I claimed the window seat and kept an eye out for Ruben. Damn, no charging point. The train started pulling away from the station. Not good! Where is Ruben?

I decided to get a cup of tea and see if I could find a charging point in the dining carriage. Excellent result, tea and charge.

It took the longest ten minutes to charge my phone. I desperately tried calling Ruben but had really bad signal.

After forty-five minutes, I heard a ping and received a message:

From: Ruben
To: Iris
Time: 9:50 a.m.
> Abort the plan. This is not a drill.
> My computer was hacked. Everything wiped and stolen.
> 3-21-12

Oh great. What does 3-21-12 mean? Puzzles never were my strong point. Ruben knew that.

I noticed a man wearing a black hoodie, watching me three seats away, across the aisle. I hadn't taken that much notice of him until now. I was consumed with fear. My stomach was in knots. Am I being followed? Am I in danger? Why do I have to abort the plan? A bit more detail would be nice. I'm not in Bletchley Park.

Pull yourself together, Iris. What would your grand-mother have done? Think and fast! I kept telling myself.

I decided to stay calm and continue reading my mag-azine whilst keeping an eye on the man across the aisle. Meanwhile, wondering what 3-21-12 meant. Is it a rhyme? All the numbers equal three. Does that mean something? Three bears, three pigs? Or am I meant to add them up? Is it nine? Do I get off at the 9th stop? Is it the square root? Am I meant to meet him in a square in Brussels? That can't be right. He said abort the plan, and he didn't know I hadn't received his message. OK, let's look at this logically. I once read that people use numbers in replace of the alphabet. Let's try 3 = C, 21 = U, 12 ah that's it. C U 12:00. He'll still meet me at 12:00 at Kurt's.

I replied to Ruben with the numbers 3-21-12. Then quickly turned off my Bluetooth to make sure my phone couldn't be hacked. I got up casually, left my magazine open, and tea next to it. I slowly walked towards the bathroom, giving the impression I'd be back shortly. At the next stopped I jumped off the train, hid behind a huge advert making sure the man in black didn't see me. I waited for two other trains to Brussels to pass, then got on the third.

I arrived in Brussels on the right side of time. Still cautious of every man in a black hoodie, which I admit, there are many in winter. Luckily, I managed to get a taxi very quickly. Arriving, surprisingly on time to Kurt's office.

I couldn't believe my eyes as we pulled up. There waiting for me at the entrance was Ruben. He gave me the biggest hug. I burst into tears.

"How did you get here?" I asked. "Have you been here long?"

"I tried desperately to get hold of you," Ruben said.

"Isaac, let me borrow a company car. I got here about fifteen minutes ago."

"What happened to your computer?" I asked.

"I'll tell you all about it later. I don't want to keep Kurt waiting. He doesn't have a lot of time." Ruben replied as we walked towards the building.

The KB Logistics building was spectacular. Comprising elegant neo-futuristic architecture with sixty storeys of reflective glass, combining modern functionality with ecological design. As we walked into the foyer, we were astonished to find an atrium filled with tropical plants and an oak tree reaching to what looked like the 3rd floor. It had the most welcoming atmosphere and an impressive timeline outlining the progression from when the business started in 1967.

Just as we'd finished reading the history, Kurt met us at reception and invited us to the boardroom on the 58th floor.

"Welcome to Brussels," he said. "It's a pleasure to meet you. My brother gave me a brief description of why you're here and your desire to learn more about Communication Intelligence and my understanding of the Fourth Dimension in Communication. Can I get you a drink?" he offered as we entered the boardroom.

"Yes, please, just a white tea for me," I replied.

"I'll have the same," said Ruben.

"I believe you already have the first section of the diary and understand it's been kept a secret, for fear of the contents being used for evil, as it was during the Second World War," Kurt began.

"Yes, Jorgen Jensen at Westerbork mentioned people were radicalised during the war. Can you explain why the contents have continued to remain secret?" I asked.

"The Fuhrer cult was a phenomenon never before seen in history. Germans had an unconditional belief in Hitler. He had become like a drug to the people, and his words became gospel. The power of his words and propaganda were the psychological basis of Hitler's popularity and influence."

"Do you know about any of the other sections?" Ruben enquired.

"I can confirm there are five sections to the diary outlining the principles of Communication Intelligence," Kurt said with a nod. "The sections focus on the Fourth Dimension in Communication. I'm told in the actual diary there is a final segment that connects all the other sections."

"Do you know why they split up the sections?" I asked, confused.

"Shortly after Westerbork was liberated on the 12th April 1945, the five sections were given in trust to people associated with Westerbork. The author and chairman of the secret meetings resolved five people would become the guardian of one principle each. They made a promise not to reveal the names of the other guardians."

"If five people became the guardian of a principle, what happened to the original diary?" I asked, bewildered at the extent to keep the contents secret.

"My father was given principle two on Empathy which I'm told you have a copy," Kurt said. "Nobody I am aware of knows what happened to the original diary or the final segment."

"Did your father use the principles of the diary?" I asked.

"For a long time after the war, the people of Holland went through a slow, healing process. The government spent a vast amount of money on reconstruction and a rejuvenation programme. I was only twelve at the end of the war and helped as much as I could around the farm. As time went on, I simply forgot about the diary. I moved to Brussels in the late 1960s and started my logistics business."

"Have you used the contents of the diary in your business?" Ruben asked.

Kurt nodded. "As my business grew, I needed help from a communication perspective and found the notes in the old bunker. I implemented these ideas to great success."

"Did you ever try to find the other sections?" I asked. "Your brother said you were fascinated by the diary."

Kurt nodded again and replied, "In 2007, my son Theo became obsessed with the idea of finding the other principles in the diary. He discovered the next section was given to Hans Bokman, an accountant who moved to London with his wife Tina. Hans was a delightful man, but his son Hans junior was overindulged and became extremely spoilt. Hans Jr. being an only child, learnt to manipulate his parents, owed everyone money and was continually being bailed out by his mother. He fought continuously with his father, who eventually died of a heart attack at aged fifty-six . Hans Jr. met an Argentinian girl at university. It turns out her grandfather had been a German guard at Auschwitz. Maria and Hans Jr. eventually married and now live in Birmingham. He owns an industrial fabrication company."

Ruben and I looked at each other in shock. Could it be the same man Bogdan works for? The man who worked for Isaac and took photos of us in the café in Oxford?

"So, what else did Theo find out?" I asked eagerly.

"Sadly, not much else. Theo was killed in a head-on collision when he was twenty-six years old. The driver of the other car was sending a text message when he smashed into Theo's car. It broke my heart to turn his life-support off, only twenty-four hours after the collision."

"Oh, I'm so sorry to hear that," I said. "My heart goes out to you. I lost my husband ten years ago; I truly understand the depth of your pain and sorrow."

"I'm sure Theo would be delighted to know you're finishing his mission and passion," Kurt said with anguish and heartache in his voice.

I nodded and gave him a sympathetic smile. "Thank you," I said. "Can you tell me how you use empathy in your business?"

Kurt nodded. "Communication is about connection. The answer to effective communication requires understanding how to connect with the listener. We teach here: 'Information is giving out; communication is getting through.' In the first section, you learnt about awareness. Awareness is all around you. Awareness is not just about yourself and your beliefs. It includes awareness of the environment, awareness of possibilities, awareness of what you're trying to achieve and most importantly awareness of your listener."

"How did you start focussing on empathy in the workplace?" Ruben asked.

"I realised very quickly when I began employing a diverse workforce from all over Europe that: *People won't remember what you said, but they will remember how you made them feel.*"

"Can you tell us how you communicate empathy to your employees?" I asked, intrigued.

"I realised taking an interest in my staff made all the difference. I give them a voice. I let them know their thoughts and opinions matter to me and the business. If they have a concern, they can raise this with me and I'll take them seriously rather than them complaining to others and poisoning the rest of the staff."

"You've been in business for over forty years. Have you seen much change in employees and their empathy levels?" Ruben asked.

"We're currently in the midst of rapid social change and empathy expansion, which in turn is creating deeper and more meaningful lives."

"In what way are we experiencing empathy expansion?" I asked, totally lost.

"Influential thinkers and philosophers have for the past 300 years been highlighting our self-interest and self-preserving tendencies to pursue our individual needs. The 'Me Generation' of self-obsession reached historical heights in the 1970s. Today, simplistic aspirations of looking after number one are as outdated as the Nokia 3310 mobile phone."

"Are you saying we're moving away from the 'Me Generation'?" Ruben said, trying to clarify.

"Let me explain what our training modules cover," Kurt said. "Empathy expansion has seen three waves since the 18th Century. The Reading Revolution caused the first wave and created the Age of Reason which saw an intellectual movement focus on reason, individualism, and scepticism. Education and the increase in reading had an enormous impact on humanities ability to feel the pain and pleasure of others, leading to a rise in awareness of humanitarian injustices and subsequent activism. As a result, we saw a decline in slavery, improving children's conditions, reducing judicial torture, and the persecution of minorities. The second wave of empathy expansion occurred after the Second World War. As the atrocities of the Holocaust were finally exposed, along with the disclosure of Hitler's suspension of the most basic civil and human rights. We saw a post-war explosion of humanitarian organisations and social groups, including rights for women, the disabled and ethnic and religious minority groups."

"When did the third wave start?" I asked. I was in total awe of his insight.

"Since the global pandemic in 2020, we've experienced the third wave in empathy expansion," Kurt continued. "During this time, we underwent prolonged periods of forced isolation. Remote working, led to many being overcome with previously unheard-of daily challenges and frustrations. Many cohabiting people found unique ways to accept, respect and support each other in confined spaces, redefining territories and house rules. This period highlighted the vast difference in technical ability of personnel, often creating insecurity in older generations and annoyance and frustration in the younger generations. It also humanised the employee. Through Zoom or conference calling the workplace façade was removed to reveal the real person behind the job title. For many the isolation caused or triggered stress and anxiety. Awareness and acceptance of mental health concerns enabled more honesty and openness about feelings, needs and support. The ability to show vulnerability and question outdated workplace practices has seen a surge in assertive behaviour to confront workplace discrimination, sexual harassment and mental health concerns."

"Have you seen any changes from the third wave in your business?" Ruben enquired.

"I believe as we're becoming more emotionally liberated and educated, we're simultaneously moving away from being an empathy deficit society. The result of the third wave of empathy expansion has seen a torrent of much needed humanitarian awareness and activism, as seen with Black Lives Matters, Climate Change, Racial Justice, LGBTQ, women's safety, and many other causes for diversity and inclusion. This in turn, has had a massive effect on the business as we know it."

"Could you explain the importance of empathy in your future business?" Ruben asked.

"We've noticed in the past five years, companies across nearly every industry are reconfiguring their businesses for the digital age, in particular artificial intelligence, augmented reality and training with virtual reality. We believe we're just at the beginning of the most fundamental business transformation in history, with humans and machines working alongside each other in ways never before thought possible."

"I'm a bit confused," I said. "What does empathy have to do with artificial intelligence?"

"We're currently moving through a period of rapid technological change, resulting in new forms of, and skills in, communication. Almost daily, we're forced to learn new methods to interact with machines and humans, such as conference calls, instant messages, and acceptable communication protocols on social media. What people don't realise is that the science and technology behind most new technology already incorporates the Fourth Dimension in Communication."

"I'm really confused, Kurt," I said, shaking my head. "How does the Fourth Dimension in Communication explain empathy?"

"Our training programme highlights the evolution of our thought processes. We initially used the stars to navigate, then progressed to a static map. Not too long ago, the first generation of GPS was introduced, which was basically a digital version of a paper map. The second-generation GPS incorporated the ability to put in a location and get directions. This was still a static process. The latest GPS apps include real-time data, using the driver's location, speed, surrounding traffic, accidents, and other obstructions to give the driver alternatives routes. We increasingly see artificial intelligence incorporating the Fourth Dimension in Communication, that is time and space in their communication models."

"How does that apply to humans?" Ruben asked, perplexed.

"We believe the answer to our communication success and empathy lies in parallel to machine learning software which incorporates, behavioural science, psychology, social science and computer science. Machines currently cannot be empathetic. However, they can read surrounding environments, analyse patterns, notice changes in behaviour, and learn to adjust and improve. Humans would become more empathetic if they learnt to read the environment and people. Asking questions such as—is this an appropriate time and place to chat? Are you in a public space? Can the person hear over all the noise? Is there a pattern of being late? Has the person suddenly withdrawn? Asking these types of question will go a long way to improving empathy in communication."

"I see, that makes a lot of sense," I said. I was rationalising in my head what Kurt just told us. "How can I form a new habit and become more empathetic?" I asked. "Is there some further reading you could recommend?"

"Empathy is like learning a new language," Kurt said. "You can read, research and repeat words and phrases but to perfect a new language, you can't beat immersing yourself in the culture, interacting and conversing with native speakers. Lessons are best learnt through experience:

You read, and you forget,

You hear, and you understand,

You experience and you remember."

"Thank you, Kurt, again that makes a lot of sense. Is there anything else you can suggest we need to do to improve our empathy?" I asked.

"There is only one very tiny new habit that will instantly transform your success in communication and deepen your relationships," Kurt said.

"Really, I can instantly change, with no lengthy study, no exams, no degree, no need to practise?" I asked sceptically.

"Yes, absolutely. The best way to improve your empathy is to ask relevant questions and patiently wait for the answer. The key is to take the time to listen to your audience. You will discover people are usually very cautious when you start asking questions; they are working out if they can trust you."

"So, how do you get around the trust element?" I asked.

"I find I only need to ask four magic questions that work every single time, which reveals the golden nugget answer and opens the door to empathy," Kurt said.

"What are these simple questions?" I asked, unconvinced. Kurt smiled and replied:

What do you think?

What else?

What else?

What else?"

"That's it, that's all I have to ask?" I said, still doubtful.

"Yes. It's known as the Golden Rule in Communication—communicate with others as you would have them communicate with you. People will want to communicate with you when you make it comfortable for them to do so. When you ask someone to do something, tell the person why, don't let the person feel uncertain of your meaning and jump to a conclusion. Answer a question directly and elaborate, and if appropriate ask a question to make sure the listener understood your answer."

Just then, Kurt's secretary came in to tell him he had a client waiting for him in reception.

"Thank you once again, Kurt; we cannot thank you enough for your openness and generosity. I feel you have truly touched and impacted our lives," I said as we left the boardroom.

The drive back to Amsterdam was a lot more pleasant than the train. For a long time, Ruben and I sat in silence. Deep in thought recounting all that had transpired during the day.

Could it be that simple to transform our skills in communication? To deepen relationships, to remove miscommunication and misunderstanding? It made a lot of sense. Awareness is the key to Empathy. If only we'd been aware of the Fourth Dimension in Communication ten years ago, perhaps Kurt's son Theo would still be alive today. The other driver would have thought twice about communicating behind the wheel and realised there was a better time and place.

Coming back to reality, I suddenly realised Ruben hadn't told me what happened to his computer this morning.

CHAPTER 6

MONDAY, 9 P.M.

Ruben's computer hacking story turned out to be a bit of an anticlimax after all we'd been through the last couple of days.

Luckily it was Ruben's personal computer which had been hacked, not his work one. However, it probably would have been better if it *was* his work one; it's encrypted and more inaccessible. Cybercriminals had sent an email via social media suggesting Ruben check out a web link that allowed access to his computer. This then opened many doors on his laptop. Luckily, he'd made a backup of the photos in Mr Solomon's tin. It's still unsettling to know that someone has the details from Mr Solomon and the first section of the diary.

o o o

I was excited to get back home to tell the girls all about what had happened in Amsterdam and Belgium. I couldn't wait to tell them about their great grandparents in Wester-bork. However, remembering what I'd learnt from Kurt, I decided to take a different approach. Instead of launching into my story the second they walked through the door from camping. I turned the kettle on, turned the television off, put my phone on silent and shut my computer.

"Hi girls, how was camping?" I asked. "Would you like a hot chocolate and a slice of banana loaf?"

"Yep, camping was good," they replied and started walking towards their room.

When they came back, I asked, "Tell me, what did you have to do on the trip?" whilst clearing the table.

"We had to hike up a mountain in the Peak District and sleep in the freezing cold," Miranda said. She then turned to walk away again.

"Oh, your father would be so proud of you," I said. My words stopped her from walking away. "Tell me about your orienteering." I gestured for the girls to join me at the table. "Where did you hike?"

They both made their way to the table. Melody began to open up: "Oh my god, it was so funny. We decided to take a shortcut through a field and came up close and personal with an angry cow. We had to leg it over some hay bales and then over a prickly fence. That's when Emma twisted her ankle." Melody smirked.

"Poor Emma," I said. "What happened?"

"Well, because we weren't allowed a phone, we had to help her until we were busted for going through some farmer's field. Luckily that didn't take too long," Miranda replied whilst taking a massive chunk of banana loaf. "Actually, I did have my phone in case of an emergency, but they didn't know that. If it had taken much longer, I would have used my phone," Miranda added rather confidently. "Isn't that what you've always said, Mum? Never leave home without your phone, keys and a card with money on it?"

"I have the best photos of the cow; he was really shitty. Do you want to see?" Melody interjected, bubbling with excitement.

Holding my tongue, I decided not to tell them off but kept asking questions.

"So, what did your teacher say when you were busted going through the field?" I asked.

"Mr Jacob said he knew if anyone was going to take a shortcut, it would be us, so he just sat waiting in his car," Melody said, and the girls burst out laughing.

"It was so funny. We got a free lift back to base, so we didn't hold up the rest of the group," Miranda said a little too enthusiastically.

"What happened when you got to base?" I asked, worried about Emma.

"Mrs Wright felt sorry for Emma, who was giving it her best with an academy award performance and in floods of tears. Can you believe it? Mrs Wright fell for it hook line and sinker and gave her a huge brownie."

"That was nice of Mrs Wright. Lucky she'd packed the brownies. What did Mrs Wright say about your shortcut?"

"Nothing, I changed the subject quickly and pointed out that if it weren't for us taking a shortcut leading us to safety, Emma would still be in the field, probably trampled by the cow," Miranda replied without missing a beat. "Score, we got a brownie too!"

And so, the girls and I had the most wonderful afternoon. I learnt more in those three hours than I had in the past three years. We laughed until we had tears in our eyes. Thank you, Kurt.

I can now see how it's possible to make an instant change simply by asking questions and listening rather than interrupting and sabotaging a conversation with disapproving facial expressions, comments or overriding it with my own stories.

o o o

The next couple of days at work were manic, trying to play catch-up. I clicked on my emails, 352 unread messages. Note to self—unsubscribe. Pushed aside Mount Vesuvius of unopened post, scrolled down the long list of urgent calls to return, impressed only forty-seven. Decided the only way forward was a trip to the mothership for a shot of caffeine and a vanilla latte.

I received the third reminder from Clementine Jacob-Brown about the Global Mobility conference and award night, chasing me for my headshot and details of my keynote speech. Priority. Top of the list.

Human Resources still need my holiday request form.

IT need me to return cables.

Jennie in the post room needs me to sign six birthday cards.

Urgent emails—High Priority

From: Melody

To: Mum

Can you take Stewit the rabbit to the vet? He ate a candle.

From: Ruben

To: Iris

Any ideas on how we'll get Section 3?

From: Iris

To: Ruben

No idea. However, you're not going to believe it. Bokman Fabrication has been shortlisted for a Global Mobility award. I wasn't the judge.

From: Ruben

To: Iris

OMG!!! Do you think it's the right time and place to speak to him? Saves a trip to Birmingham?

From: Iris

To: Ruben

No, absolutely not. Got too much to do and too much going on. Any other suggestions?

From: Ruben

To Iris

Here's a crazy idea. .... Why don't you speak to Han's mother Tina? I just emailed Kurt he said he believes she lives in Hemel Hempstead. Not too far from you.

From: Iris

To: Ruben

Yes—that could work. Tina must have known my grandparents, wasn't she also in Westerbork? Brilliant idea. You're a genius. Thanks.

o   o   o

Tracking down Tina Bokman proved to be a bit of a challenge. She wasn't on Facebook. I couldn't find her on LinkedIn or any other social media. I suppose I'm not surprised, she's probably in her 80s or 90s. Then out of the blue, I had a breakthrough in the most surprising place. I'd popped in to see my elderly neighbour Olive for a cup of tea and to bring her post. As I was rambling about the difficulty of finding people in the Digital Age, she looked at me with a bewildered look on her face.

"But why don't you look her up in the phone book?" Olive said, clearly thinking I'd lost my marbles not to have thought of such a simple solution.

"Oh my god, yes. Have you got one?" I asked, delighted with the simplicity.

"No, petal, you have to go to where she lives and find the phone book in the post office," Olive said, looking over her reading glasses.

"Oh, right. Yes, I remember the days of the phone book," I said, feeling stupid. "Thanks."

It didn't take long to find Tina Bokman in Hemel Hampstead. I couldn't believe it, not only did I find her phone number but also her address. How easy was that? I rang Tina that afternoon and arranged to meet at 11 a.m. the next day.

o o o

Armed with a beautiful bunch of multicoloured tulips and a packet of Dutch biscuits, I felt excited to meet with Tina Bokman. Yet, just as I was about to ring the doorbell, I was suddenly filled with doubt. What if she doesn't want to talk about the war like my grandparents because it brings back so many horrific memories? What if she gets all defensive about Hans Jr.? What *am* I doing?

Just as I was beginning to totally doubt my decision, a small delicate woman with white curly hair, immaculately dressed in a tartan skirt and soft blue cable knit sweater, answered the door.

"Hello dearie, you must be Iris, come in," said Tina Bokman, smiling broadly.

The sound of her voice brought back floods of memories. I was astounded by how much she resembled my grandmother. She had the same thick Dutch accent and inflexions in her speech patterns.

"You'll have to excuse the untidy state of my home. I don't get many visitors these days," Tina said whilst leading me through her entrance hall.

I could smell and hear the coffee percolator in the kitchen.

"Come into the drawing-room and make yourself comfortable while I get the coffee," she said.

I couldn't believe my eyes. Tina's house had the same carpet on the table, the same heavy wooden furniture and grandfather clock that chimes every half hour. She even had crocheted doilies on the armrest of her sofa. I felt like I'd time-warped back to the 1980s and to my grandparents' home.

Talking to Tina proved inspiring. Her memory was as sharp as a tack. Not only did she remember my grandparents and her time in Westerbork, but she also knew my mother personally.

"My husband and I lived next door to your grandparents," Tina explained. "We entered Westerbork as prisoners in 1943. Your grandfather employed my husband, Hans Sr, as an accountant and office manager. We were considered essential workers, which prevented our names from being put on the daily list to go on the trains to the extermination camps. We are eternally grateful to your grandparents and owe our lives to them. I would be delighted to help in any way I can."

"Did you have an opportunity to spend time with my grandmother?" I asked, brimming with pride.

"Yes, in fact, I ended up working for your grandmother. Sadly, her nanny's name went on the list, she and her twin sister were deported to Auschwitz. It broke your grandmother's heart. She'd just given birth to your Aunt Anneke. I stepped in and became your grandmother's nanny until liberation."

"I can't believe you knew my mother as a small child, and my aunt. What was my mother like?" I said. I was fascinated by the unfolding of events.

"I can see you take after your mother," Tina said with a smile. "You have the same strength and determination. I couldn't take my eye off her for a second. She constantly ran off and escaped to play with the other children who were prisoners. She frightened the life out of me one day when she nearly ended up on a deportation train. How is she?"

"Unfortunately, she had a stroke and passed away a few years ago," I said.

"I'm so sorry," Tina said with heartfelt sadness.

"It's OK," I replied with a small smile.

"Did you realise your grandmother was a schoolteacher and helped children in the camp with their Dutch language and literature?" Tina continued. "She would return from her resistance work with books from the outside, to help young children with their reading. She was extremely sensitive to the children's trauma and anxiety. She delicately praised their efforts, encouraged making mistakes whilst nurturing and boosting their morale."

"I didn't know that," I said, feeling embarrassed. "She must have been very busy doing resistance work, looking after two small children and teaching."

"She was, we all were. With all the hardship and misery in the camp, we desperately tried to help the young and vulnerable." Tina nodded. "Yes, and your grandmother went out of her way to make time for the orphaned children. She understood their loss and made every effort to get to know them individually. She knew how to ask the right questions to get them to open up and express their true selves. She knew how to excite the children about learning. The children loved it when they read fables and character-building stories with values, morals, and universal truths. Your grandmother would cleverly ask questions such as—Was it right for Goldilocks to enter the bears' house without permission? Was it OK for her eat the bears' food and break their furniture?"

Tina paused and smiled as she recalled. "The object was to get the children to think, to use not only book knowledge but common sense," she explained. "Your grandmother had an uncanny ability to ignite the children's full mental, and psychological powers of thinking, problem-solving and learning. As a direct result of her teaching and getting through to them on an emotional level, these often-naughty children learnt how to respond to kindness and became more confident in themselves. I've heard from close family and friends many of these children later excelled in school and became hugely successful bankers, doctors, pharmacists, lawyers, musicians and very famous in Hollywood. I believe this was all because your grandmother knew the secrets to get through to people and building relationships. She taught them the love of learning."

I felt tears welling in my eyes. I had no idea she had done all this.

"Did your grandmother teach after the war?" Tina asked.

"No, unfortunately, when my grandparents moved to Australia, she got tuberculosis and never worked again," I said. "It's interesting though, my sister Bianca, who is the most like my grandmother, followed in her footsteps and went into teaching, well, training. My grandmother must have passed on her knowledge because Bianca is head of training for a global IT solutions company. She's been there for fifteen years and has had the most amazing career progression. I've always been in awe of her patience and her skills in relationship building."

"I wish I could say the same for my son Hans Jr.," Tina said with a sigh. "We had him quite late and gave him everything he ever wanted. After witnessing the atrocities of the war, we wanted him to have the best and to never suffer. Looking back, I'm not sure that was the right thing to do."

"In what way?" I asked boldly.

"Hans was a very bright student and excelled at maths. We were very proud of him. He always had a quick wit and sharp eye. You'd find it difficult to find a more charming, polished young man. An accomplished, smooth talker. He loves the best in life, but unlike his father, he doesn't like hard work," Tina replied with sadness in her voice.

"I'm sorry to hear that," I said. I was looking down, unsure if this was the right moment to ask about the secret diary.

"Mrs Bokman," I asked, before briefly hesitating. "I know this may sound a bit random. But while you were in Westerbork, did you ever hear of a secret diary that was being written on the Fourth Dimension in Communication?" I crossed my fingers and toes, hoping she had.

With a look of shock on her face and a long pause—I think she was trying to decide if she could trust me—she said, "Yes, dearie, I did. We made a solemn promise when we were in the camp not to mention or discuss the diary until we believed with all our heart it would be safe."

Tina paused to collect herself. Taking a deep breath, she continued: "As I shared the most traumatic time in my life with your grandparents in Westerbork, I believe it will be OK to impart what I know. But first, would you like a cup of tea and a biscuit, dear? I just need a few moments to find my notes which are in an old suitcase. When we left the camp Hans Sr, and I packed our entire life in a small suitcase and turned our back on the past. I won't be long."

"Would you like some help?" I offered.

"That would be lovely, pet," said Mrs Bokman.

We took a break from our conversation to have tea and a biscuit, then went up to Tina's bedroom to search for the notes. We found the old leather suitcase she'd mentioned with a worn leather strap covered in dust under the bed.

Going through the suitcase proved to be quite an emotional journey for Mrs Bokman. The bag contained old photos, ID cards, a notebook with receipts and a list of neatly written accounts, a pencil and many other treasures, including a newspaper from the day of liberation. Mrs Bokman took her time, carefully turning over all the forgotten items, reading notes, and closely examining all her memories with tears welling in her eyes.

Finally, hidden in the middle of the newspaper, we found the notes Mrs Bokman had been trying to find.

Wanting to be sensitive to Mrs Bokman and considering the flood of emotions she must be currently processing, I gently asked, "Do you mind telling me how you became the guardian of these notes?"

Mrs Bokman explained "We had regular discussions about the psychological warfare being used by the Nazis. A group of six men from different backgrounds in psychology, physics, engineering, accounting, sales, and a teacher met weekly to discuss their ideas. I would act as a secretary and make notes. But I only took notes for the section we later became the guardian of."

Mrs Bokman then carefully showed me the notes.

What I saw was simply amazing. The Bokmans had perfectly preserved the notes from 1944 and elegantly captured time and history.

"Can you tell me what they discussed in these meetings?" I enquired in awe of her time capsule.

"Our discussions were delightfully diverse due to the input from experts from a vast range of backgrounds," Tina began. "Their level of skill was incredible. Due to their varied knowledge and experience they were each able to observe a different dimension to challenges we faced within the camp."

"Did these men know each other before the war?" I asked, thrilled to be learning so much.

"Some of the men knew each other, but not all of them. The one thing they had in common was their astounding careers before the war. They were all very well connected, including knowing Albert Einstein and Wilhelm Wundt."

"Who is Wilhelm Wundt?" I asked naively.

"Wilhelm Wundt was the father of experimental psychology and behavioural studies. He led the way in quantifying behaviour by direct observation. He used stimulus and response experiments and spent a vast amount of time researching the relationship between the inner and outer world."

"I can't believe the men in the camp had access to such brilliant minds. Was there anyone else that influenced them? I asked.

"Let me clarify," Tina said, very carefully. "These men didn't have access to these famous men during the war. They knew them before the war. One of the other men in our meetings had also known Theodore Newcomb. We spent a lot of time reflecting on Theodore's thoughts on his proposed communication model, which he subsequently published in the 1950s. We too implemented research studies to measure our success."

"How did you do that?" I asked curiously.

"We monitored several groups within the camp over a three-and-a-half-year period. A considerable amount of time and thought went into designing the studies and determining the appropriate measurement methods. It took well over twelve months for everyone to critically review and agree on how to interpret the results. We had everyone come up with potential flaws in arguments from their different industries."

"What type of behaviours did you study?" I asked, totally engrossed in our conversation.

"We studied objective observation, implicit and explicit listening, and roadblocks to effective communication. These three modules included perception, interaction, collaborative problem-solving and conflict resolution."

"How did you do that with the camp inmates?" I asked. I was confused at the enormity of the study.

"Each group of inmates studied focused on a particular theory. We had a control group with no special interaction and an associated group getting a specified form of interaction. We even included silence as a form of interaction."

"What did you do with all the information and measurements from the study?"

"We monitored and measured all the responses very carefully," Tina replied. "Using a comprehensive manual statistical analysis process, we came up with the principles of Communication Intelligence incorporating the Fourth Dimension in Communication. We didn't have computers or software programmes back then. I remember my husband Hans staying up late doing the mathematical calculations. It gave him such joy and happiness."

I asked, "Did anyone criticise or complain about what you were doing?"

"No, we made sure all experiments were completely anonymous, so it didn't affect the results. As you can imagine," Mrs Bokman continued, "it was a very traumatic time in people's lives. There was a huge amount of distrust and uncertainty within the camp. We didn't want to add to people's stress and concern. Scepticism was all around us. Many in the camp had strong views and were very set in their ways. They just wanted to hang on to what they knew and what they were comfortable believing. They couldn't cope with more change and the unknown. There are still many people like that today. I, however, feel scepticism is good. It makes us work harder, be more disciplined and makes us provide even more proof of our findings."

"How did they decide on the final principles for Communication Intelligence?" I asked.

"I remember the group had many strategy meetings about the communication framework. They were all in agreement that it should be simple enough for anyone to apply without interfering with their daily lives and commitments. It should bring advancement and new depth to relationships with, family, associates, business and for the betterment of humankind."

"If the principles were for good, why were they scared to publish the results?"

"They were mindful that knowledge creates power, but possession is useless unless put to practical use. They stressed this knowledge should be for universal good, as the opposite can only lead to evil and bring destruction to those who exercise it."

"Why did they think the principles could be used for evil and cause harm?" I asked, desperately struggling to understand.

"They recognised it is easier for the majority of human-kind to act with wrongdoing," Tina explained. "Goodwill requires hard work and discipline. To overcome being drawn towards evil, criticism, judgement, gossip, and manipulation requires energy, focus, courage and effort— *'The first step and most important victory is to conquest the self. There is no light without shadow, and strength will only grow through resistance.'* "

I nodded. I was impatient to learn more but was wary of coming across as rude. I gently asked, "Do your notes out-line the third principle in Communication Intelligence?"

"Yes, my dear, they do," Tina replied, looking down at the suitcase and getting out a piece of discoloured paper.

Tina took a long deep breath and paused as if trans-porting herself back to the camp and those covert back-room meetings.

3. Interaction—The third principle in Communication Intelligence

We take inspiration from Isaac Newton and Theodore Newcombe.

This principle transforms the understanding of the Laws of Human Nature and will build heightened sensi-tivity when interacting with others.

Understanding the Principles of Interaction creates a deeper appreciation of our own emotions and those of others. We become more present in the moment. With this new level of heightened-perception, the former dull interaction becomes alive with awareness. What was previously unseen becomes visible and amazing results occur.

Just as Isaac Newton's laws of nature removed uncertainty in the world by showing the universe operates predictably, we too can demonstrate similar principles with the Laws of Human Nature.

Humans are also affected by natures' push and pull when they interact with others. All humans are susceptible to the emotions and moods of those around them, compelling an unconscious response of either imitating others, getting caught up in their dramas, reacting and responding depending on the interaction. Humans, in general, tend to respond in predictable ways.

There are many laws and principles when interacting with others. Understanding the basic principles of reciprocity, authority, congruency, likability and crowd psychology will create deeper, more satisfying bonds and lasting relationships.

I sat in silence for quite a while, trying to take it all in.

Mrs Bokman broke my silence by placing her hand on my shoulder. "Amazing, isn't it? So simple and logical once it's broken down."

"It certainly is," I agreed. "Did you use these principles in your life?"

"I certainly did," she replied. "For many years, I worked in Human Resources, in my husband's accountancy firm

Bokman Cohen Silver. We had offices all over the world. As time went on, I learnt to read people as well as reading a book. This made for very fluid conversations and delightful, trusting relationships. When Hans Sr passed away, we sold his share in the business. I needed something to keep me busy, so I became a life coach and successfully passed on my knowledge to my clients."

"Do you think it's easy to learn to read people?" I asked.

"Yes, indeed. We already read people and don't realise it. Growing up with TV and theatre has taught us these skills. When watching a scene unfold on TV, we're 100% focussed on the situation. When engaged in a conversation, we're too busy coming up with a response to acknowledge the other person and external cues. As information comes to us, our mind is making assumptions and jumping ahead. Trust me. We do not need to unlock dormant receptors, study neuroscience or become an expert in body language. We simply need to be quiet and take in the scene."

I looked at her, puzzled, and she returned my gesture with a reassuring smile. "Usually, the simplest solutions are staring us in the face; we simply have to look in the right direction."

I drove home on autopilot, my head spinning with all this new information. Mrs Bokman very kindly let me take photos of her notes. She also said I was most welcome to come back anytime. She said she'd love to hear more about my grandparents and mother and would be very happy to discuss my progress using the principle of 'Interaction'. I couldn't stop smiling; and had an overwhelming sense of connection and felt a deep sense of love and kindness.

As I walked out the door, Tina placed a small gift in my hands and told me to open it when I got home.

CHAPTER 7

Returning to the office, I leapt straight into a frantic afternoon of multitasking, checking my phone, emails, WhatsApp, and a sneaky glance every now and then on social media. I admit I live on an addictive diet of trashy news and gossipy social media. Far too often, I find myself sucked into a black hole of spontaneous (but very thorough) Facebook stalking; a quick scroll somehow turns into a full-on stalk of an old classmate who's lost two stone (seriously jealous). Before you know it, I'm deep down another rabbit-hole. How can that be possible? I've just lost thirty-five minutes. No, it can't be. But it was so worth it. I just found out that my old classmate broke up with her boyfriend and has recently returned from Portugal with her girlfriends. Wow, not sure if that new short haircut was a good idea. She now works for a start-up that established in 2019. She's delighted to be focussing on her career right now.

I do love these constant distractions; it gets me through an otherwise tedious day.

It seems like most of my days, however, are fuelled by stress and caffeine. A week ago, I took off my watch. My reasoning was if I stop looking at my watch, I'll feel less overwhelmed. I then reconfigured my time management schedule, only to discover that the more I structured my time, the more I crammed into my day.

I can honestly say I'm living in the epicentre of the rat race. At the end of most days, I'm completely depleted, with little energy to make clear, strategic decisions or give adequate advice. My busy footprint would leave the most ardent carbon footprint warrior in the depths of despair.

I discovered that my biggest vice is social media. Like the latest Dyson vacuum cleaner, it sucks the life out of my day. Social media has been fantastic in growing my friends and connections exponentially whilst simultaneously reducing my communication's depth and sincerity to those at the shallow end of the gene pool. I'm exhausted trying to maintain all these platforms and relationships. I suffer daily bouts of guilt and shame when reminded *again* (shame on whoever invented the phone reminder) to update my profile, post relevant content and funny images. Thanks to the latest marketing trends, I'm now expected to create a personal brand, which means scripting, staging and filming an engaging two-to-three-minute video for YouTube. Oh my god!

Priority list:

- Check emails
- Update Ruben

- Return client calls
- Departmental meeting
- Work on files

From: Iris
To: Ruben

Hey Rubes, I had the most fantastic time with Mrs Bokman. Got loads to tell. Are you free tonight to chat?

I xx

PS so sweet she gave me a little gift when I left. Still haven't had a chance to open it.

From: Ruben
To: Iris

Sure, sounds like a plan. 8:30 p.m., OK?

From Iris:
To Ruben:

Perfect ☺ xx

From: Donna Walsh (Elliott Migration)
To: Iris De Angelo (Global Visas)

Hey Hon, I just found out that the man you mentioned, Hans Bokman, has a student (Grad scheme/ Overseas work experience) event in London tonight. It's just around the corner from my work. I know it's short notice. Do you want to check out the event then have a bite to eat?

D xx

From Iris De Angelo (Global Visas)
To: Donna Walsh (Elliott Migration)
Absolutely ☺ What time does it start? How much is it?
I xx

From: Donna Walsh (Elliott Migration)
To: Iris De Angelo (Global Visas)
6:30 p.m., it's free. Want to meet me at my office at
6:10 p.m. and go together?
D xx

From: Iris De Angelo (Global Visas)
To: Donna Walsh (Elliott Migration)
Yep. See you 6:10 p.m. xx

Donna and I met ten years ago at a sponsored migration event. Suppliers regularly hold events to encourage lawyers and migration agents to refer their clients to them for accommodation, removals, pet relocation, opening bank accounts, tax, pensions, and the like.

We love going; the organisers have done all the hard work getting our friends in the industry together. It's usually in the most highly sought after new venue, with endless wine, champagne and nibbles. They are always very well attended.

Donna and I arrived at The Strand across from the Australian High Commission to find a crowd of students waiting to enter. There was much excitement in the air. As we entered the auditorium, we heard playing on the loudspeaker 'We Are the Champions' by Queen. The atmosphere was buzzing. Students were pushing to get to the front. We turned to see Hans Bokman Jr. entering the building. Before him were several men with mics attached to their head, clearing a path for him to walk through the masses. Hans touched people's shoulders along the way, then stretched his arms up to the sky like a pseudo-religious leader when he walked onto the stage. The crowd roared and clapped with delirious enthusiasm.

Donna and I just looked at each other, dumbfounded. We were speechless by the extraordinary magnetism of his appeal. "What's going on?" Donna asked, clearly confused by the mayhem.

"Beats me," I said. "I thought the guy had some sort of metal fabrication business up in Birmingham."

"I checked out his website before we left," Donna said. "It said something about climate change, they'd invented some whizzbang new filter that seems to clean industrial pollution and wastewater or something."

Just then, Bogdan walked on the vast stage and introduced Hans Jr. It was immediately apparent that a phenomenal team was behind this emotion-driven, image-building machine.

With precision and rehearsed gestures, Hans walked with deliberate long, slow strides across the stage. I was taken by how tall he was, over six feet, with broad shoulders and an imposing manner.

He presented as a devilishly handsome man with a charming smile capable of melting the most sinister of spinsters. He was dressed conservatively in a Savile Row bespoke suit accompanied by a very expensive pair of Oxford shoes.

The crowd below looked up with stars in their eyes. Hans' words came across as gospel. He injected hope and inspiration into the enthusiastic band of loyal disciples. His carefully scripted words brought forth a tide of admiration, awe and aspiration for a new future.

His message painted him as the saviour of the 'lost generation' who were suffering and falling between the pandemic gaps. He articulated and legitimised their grievances. He applauded their demands for justice and opportunity. He had undoubtedly nominated himself as the leader and authority for the new generation. He would save these young people and give them the opportunities they so desperately deserved and desired. He had an unfailing appeal as a speaker. He elaborated on the depth of the economic crisis, the hardship of the young, and the ideals they fiercely fought for. His charismatic style was unfathomable. He created a pendulum of emotional triggers from fear and despair to euphoria and utopian hopes for a prosperous future. He was their only hope for the future.

I was awestruck. The stage management was brilliantly choreographed, exploiting Hans' natural delivery style, building on his unshakable confidence. Without a doubt, his delivery strengthened the audience's morale, giving hope to a new generation of young people transitioning into the workforce. He promised eternal happiness, freedom and opportunity.

The grand finale of this faultless show was a spectacular opportunity for the right candidate. Hans held up a beautifully designed, expensive-looking, high-gloss brochure, with liberal sprinklings of millennials working remotely (mostly poolside). There were breath-taking images of exotic locations (perfect for taking selfies). Pictures of young people and their adorable pugs, working and living in a penthouse (with a heated pool). Of course, it displayed the must-have flamingo pool floaties and personal trainer.

With precision in millennial terms, it read: "This job is 'totally worthwhile'—you're guaranteed to work the hours of your choice. It's a once in a lifetime opportunity to work where you feel valued and empowered. A place where you can fulfil your life purpose and make a difference in the world."

The music started again, this time playing Queen's 'Don't Stop Me Now'. It created a wave of high energy in the young crowd. They were jumping, dancing and clapping. When Hans left the stage, the crowd went wild, running towards the registration table staffed by a balanced assortment of people from diverse backgrounds in matching black outfits. Everyone seemed to want to be the first to put in their application.

Donna and I were intrigued to read more about this fantastic job offer. The brochure said:

For only a £100 registration fee, all students have an opportunity to apply for a graduate scheme, training contract or apprenticeship with guaranteed global travel. The

£100 registration fee includes a free pack with tips and expert advice, giving students inside knowledge to apply for other jobs in the industry, in the event the applicant was unsuccessful.

For all those who do not think they have the right credentials or necessary experience; Bokman Fabrication is offering to a limited number of applicants another opportunity to obtain the perfect job.

For only £3,500 (all credit cards accepted), applicants can attend a one-week course, which will make you eligible to apply for this once in a lifetime job. Places are filling fast. By registering now, you can save 50%. That means for only £1,750 you can secure your place and transform your life—forever! For any student who doesn't have the money, a loan could be arranged on the spot.

I was hooked. Give me an application form!

"Donna, I need to talk to this guy," I said, bubbling with enthusiasm. "I really like him. He raised some valid points. He certainly understands what these students are going through. I think maybe I should talk to him about the diary."

Donna took me by the arm and led me out of the auditorium.

"Let's go. Hans has you hooked," Donna said. "It sounds suspicious to me."

I was confused by her behaviour but over pizza, Donna explained what she'd recently learnt in her behavioural science degree. Since her promotion into the compliance team, Donna decided that there was no point in having all these policies and procedures if you don't have the behaviours to drive them. So off she went and enrolled in *another* degree. The girl's amazing. She's got a scholarship and has been offered a place in the PhD programme.

"Iris," she stated firmly, "this guy has used all the classic communication tricks in the book. For starters, he's targeted the most vulnerable group of young students who are desperate for an opportunity to fulfil their dreams of the good life. He's exploited their struggles, emphasising the current fractured world with the global pandemic, trade wars, Brexit and the lack of opportunities for young students entering the workforce. He's feeding and exploiting their worst fears. He's promising certainty in uncertain times."

Donna paused to take a bite of pizza. "The whole presentation was staged, using pseudo-religious ceremonial tactics," she continued fervidly. "Do you want me to run through his use of psychology?" she asked.

"Yes, I'd love to hear it," I replied, yet feeling a bit unsure.

"Let's start at the beginning. I'll only explain a couple of high impact behaviours not to overwhelm you," Donna began. "By having someone else glowingly introduce Hans, i.e. Bogdan, it raises the speaker's credibility and value. It's far superior to self-promotion. Look at reviews; people always believe the word of another over self-promotion."

"How did he get the enormous emotional support from the audience?" I asked, baffled by his magic touch.

"He planted his people in the crowd. He used them as a stooge to ask relevant leading questions with prepared answers."

"What do you mean?" I said, not sure I understood to which part of the presentation she was referring.

"Do you remember when one of Hans' staff, disguised as a student, asked, 'How bad do you think unemployment amongst under-25s is?' Then Hans replied emotionally, 'The worst in recorded history…' Hans wanted people to know the severity of these facts to make his offer more enticing. Every gesture, every movement, his deliberate use of body language and his clever choice of persuasive words all stacks up to sway his audience."

"Gosh, I hadn't viewed his presentation like that at all," I said, embarrassed. I honestly believed him. What other tricks did he use?"

"To gain the respect and admiration of his audience, he began by identifying with their mood, thoughts and pain. In this way, he builds a feeling of congruence and alignment. They believe he understands their plight and concerns. This technique is called the Law of State Transference. This was done by Hans initially matching his students' emotional state, which creates rapport on a deep, subconscious level. He then subtly changes his state slightly, speeding up his tone and voice, aspiring to a better future."

"Yes, I remember Hans doing that," I said. "Didn't he ask the audience more questions when he was getting excited about the future?"

"Yes, he asked the audience questions to get confirmation. The planted members of the audience began nodding and clapping. Then Hans asked, 'Does everyone agree?' This tactic is to gain 'the hook'. People yell out, 'Yes'. He says, 'Sorry I couldn't hear you,' they repeat, 'Yes' and again he says, 'I still can't hear you.' They yell, 'Yes!' Once the hook has been reached, Hans changes his state again, building momentum and excitement."

"I can see how that works. It happens everywhere you go, especially at concerts, to get the crowd excited," I said, feeling more enlightened.

"That's exactly right," Donna continued. "By the end of his presentation, the crowd has been swept up to absolute emotional elation. To compound the effect, he combines his awe-inspiring words with synchronised, inspirational loud music."

"I noticed that, but didn't he also add images of a sparkling future on the big screen?" I said, remembering the alluring images of idyllic beaches, a penthouse, and a crowd of young people dancing at a concert.

"He did. He left them with the images they'd been dreaming of, causing the students to be overcome with excitement. That's when they started dancing, jumping and clapping, raising the energy sky-high. At the peak of the students' hysteria, he asks them to pay."

"That's very cunning," I said, annoyed that I'd been fooled.

"It's been scientifically proven that people with a pressing need or strong desire are more susceptible to undetected influence or mind control than someone satisfied or comfortable. A manipulator knows how to confidently charm a target, create laughter, raise hopes and lower the target's guard. Through carefully chosen words, he charms the target to get the result he desires. Hans' use of strategically placed deceptive words makes the students feel as if Hans just happens to offer what they are looking for at this particular time in their life. He leads the student on a mental journey into an idealised future. He uses the student's fragile mental wellbeing, which has recently been shaken to the core through isolation, and the pandemic, to bewilder and induce them."

"I noticed nobody seemed to question him," I said, replaying Hans' delivery in my mind.

"That's because Hans was able to easily influence the students using the Laws of Human Nature."

"Which law was that?" I asked.

"We all have a natural inclination to prefer people who are similar to us. Hans influenced the students by giving details of his struggles as a student, the transformation he went through during his apprenticeship, which led to his stratospheric success. They felt he 'got them', he was 'on their side', he was 'batting for them'. All strategic steps to strengthen the bond between him and his audience."

"Well, he must have done his research; I certainly believed he was an authority and leader in his field," I said. "Did he use a unique technique to enhance his image of authority and leadership?"

"He reinforced his authority using environmental and nonverbal cues," Donna explained. "His professional attire was flawless, his walk and mannerisms exuded boundless confidence. The expensive brochure, breath-taking stock images, offering a dream job in an exotic location. All add to his charismatic, authoritative persona."

"I found the entire presentation just flowed," I said with a nod. "Every piece of information fell into place seamlessly. To the extent I was desperately thirsty for more of this addictive information."

"His use of congruency was very powerful. Hans' image, body language and external cues were all aligned. Research shows that people perceive consistency or congruency as sincerity, and consistent people are seen as more intelligent. He firmly entrenched his authority and sincerity by his clever choreographed presentation. Carl Rogers was the first to describe the match between a person's inner feelings and outer display. Inconsistency creates a feeling of discomfort and can be perceived as a threat."

"He certainly hooked me," I confessed. "What a crowd-pleaser! Is there a technique to arouse an entire crowd?" I was thinking back to what Tina had mentioned in her notes.

"He used what's known as crowd psychology," Donna explained.

"What does that mean?" I asked. I was in total awe of her very useful knowledge.

"When people are part of an organised crowd, their conscious mind is substituted by the unconscious actions of the crowd."

"Sorry, you just lost me," I said.

"All the world's masters, the founders of empires, religions and apostles have shared an instinctive knowledge of the character of crowds. Napoleon and Hitler had incredible insight into the psychology of the masses. Research has shown a gathering of individuals from whatever nationality, sex, profession or common cause, when brought together will be subjected to the Law of the Mental Unity of Crowds."

"How does this law affect individuals?" I asked, not sure I was following.

"Once in a crowd, an individual's conscious personality disappears; it seems to merge with the thoughts and feelings of the majority of the crowd."

"Does that happen to everyone?" I asked.

"The individual assumes the characteristics peculiar to the acts of the crowd and in particular, the leader. Every crowd is different, of course, depending on the age, race and composition. The intensity and excitement of the crowd also make a difference."

"Is that what Hans did?" I remembered the elation of the entire crowd.

"Yes," Donna nodded, "the fact that the young audience had merged into a crowd puts them into a collective mindset which makes them think, feel and act in a manner quite different from how they would as an individual in a state of isolation."

"Did Hans use special words to motivate the crowd into a crowd mentality?" I asked, fascinated by these laws.

"In a crowd, every sentiment and act is contagious. Don't get me wrong, there are, of course, people who have a very strong personality and can resist the suggestive forces within a crowd. However, in general, there is a disappearance of the conscious nature of the individual, which is replaced by the crowd's unconscious actions."

"Do you think people just become lazy and let the leader make all the decisions for them?" I wondered.

"Scientists have found when an individual forms part of an organised crowd, common sense descends several layers. The individual in a crowd tends to act merely on instinct and spontaneity rather than using conscious reasoning. This results in the individual being far more impressionable to words and images than he would as an isolated individual. In summary, the crowd is always intellectually inferior to the isolated individual. It does, however, depend on the nature of the suggestion to which the crowd is exposed."

I suddenly realised this is what Mrs Bokman was trying to say about interaction in the third section of the diary. Donna's analysis of Hans on stage was precisely what Mrs Bokman said about likeability, reciprocity, authority, congruency and crowd psychology. It was all starting to make a lot of sense.

The rest of the evening, Donna and I spent catching up on bog-standard gossip. I checked my messages and realised I'd forgotten about getting back to Ruben. I quickly typed out a WhatsApp message:

From: Iris
To: Ruben

Sorry Rube, no time to chat tonight. I'll touch base tomorrow at lunch and arrange a time to chat. At the

Global Mobility event all day tomorrow, then Gala award
night in the evening. Long one.

Sorry

Xx

From: Ruben

To: Iris

No worries Rissy, I totally get it. Chat tomorrow.

Xx

"Iris, you need to learn to switch off," Donna said, as I
read through my messages. I looked up. I could tell from
her expression that she was getting annoyed at me constantly looking at my phone.

"Sorry, Donna, I just got a message from Margaret
Brown," I explained. "You remember Margaret; she used
to work for the Department of Immigration. She's a real
hoot. Knows everything about everyone."

"Oh yeah, I remember her. She's the lady with the pixie
haircut. She loves wearing red."

"Listen to this..." I said as I read Margaret's WhatsApp
message.

From: Margaret Brown

To: Iris

Hi Gorgeous, want to hear some gossip about that guy
Hans Bokman. I just heard some interesting dirt, fresh of
the rumour mill?

From: Iris

To: Margaret Brown

Yes, Always!! But busy at the moment. Can it wait until before registration tomorrow morning?

From: Margaret Brown

To: Iris

Absolutely. Let's meet at the coffee bar at 8 am.

From: Iris

To: Margaret Brown

Coolio—can't wait.

CHAPTER 8

I managed to drag myself out of bed at silly o'clock. It was still pitch-black outside, cold, and—what a surprise for London—raining! I usually spend a good fifteen minutes every single morning ironing my hair. If it rains or it's humid, I'm stuffed. The minute I walk out the door, my hair instantaneously becomes curly, frizzy and totally uncontrollable. Where's my trusty wide-brimmed black hat?

"Girls, time to get up," I shout upstairs at 7 a.m. "Breakfast is ready."

The girls came stomping downstairs, phones in hand. They were transfixed on their screens.

"I need you both to come straight home after school this afternoon. Don't forget we've got the awards night. We have to leave here by 6 p.m. Sharp!"

"Sorry Mum, can't," they said in unison—a now perfected art in synchronised teenage response patterns.

"Excuse me," I said. "We arranged this weeks ago. I bought you those expensive new dresses you insisted you had to have, with the shimmer in the moonlight black satin stockings that give you the legs of a model. Not to mention the 'go anywhere' silver sparkle handbags that everyone has. All of which cost me a fortune, I might add."

"Sorry, Mum, I've got too much homework," Melody said. "I've got course work due in the morning, and it counts towards my final mark. I'm sure you don't want me to miss out on a place at uni because of the awards night?"

"What about you, Miranda?" I asked, exasperated and filled with scepticism.

"Umm, yep, me too. Got a paper due," Miranda said, looking down at her phone.

"Well, one of you has to come. I've already paid for the tickets," I said, infuriated. "Plus, I promised Clementine you'd help hand out the awards and certificates. Which, may I remind you, is going on your personal statement for your uni application. And Donna also confirmed last night Poppy is going."

"Fine, I'll go," Miranda sulked, "but that doesn't mean I want to or that I'll pretend to have a good time."

∘ ∘ ∘

I met Margaret at the coffee bar at 8 a.m. I love the fact that she's always on time, so refreshingly reliable. I could spot her as I came up the escalator, radiating in vintage glamour. She wore a 1960s psychedelic red and yellow silk Pucci caftan with a matching headscarf. She managed to effortlessly glide across the floor towards the coffee bar with her flamboyant yet graceful steps. She should have been on the stage. Never one to disappoint, she wasted no time updating me on who was doing what, who had moved organisations and which speakers not to miss at today's conference.

Keeping the best until last, she then went on to elaborate on the Hans Bokman gossip.

"I was speaking to a friend who's on the judging panel," Margaret began, looking around with caution speaking in a whisper so as not to be overheard. "As they get so many excellent applications, which seem to be professionally written," she continued, "the judges are now encouraged to do random spot checks on applicants who are new in the market place. It's a bit like mystery shopping."

"What a sensible idea," I said. "What does it have to do with Hans Bokman?"

"Hans was shortlisted for the category 'Best Talent Mobility Strategy in a Start-up' and was randomly picked for a spot-check."

"What did the mystery shopper find?" I asked with intrigue.

Margaret replied, "The judge arrived unannounced, so he could get a true reflection of the business without giving Hans time to camouflage any areas of concern."

"Did Hans realise he was being verified?" I smiled. I was thoroughly enjoying Margaret's news.

"John, the judge, pulled up to the address given by Hans in his application but felt confused when he arrived at his destination. The building before him looked absolutely nothing like the one on his website. Feeling baffled, he drove off to find the imposing building he'd seen displayed on the About Us page with his vibrant young team."

"That's weird? What happened?"

"After ten minutes, he gave up and went back to where he started. He decided to go to reception and see if this was Bokman Fabrication. To his annoyance, it was. Hans had used a stock photo and photoshopped his staff in front of the building. As you can imagine, John instantly felt deceived and wondered what else Hans had lied about in his application."

"What was it like inside?"

"John noticed the reception area had damp rising in the corners and paint peeling off the walls. The poor girl at reception was in front of Intel ATX 2.1 computer."

"Sorry, a what?" I asked, confused.

"It's one of the computers released around 2002. I remember using one back in the early noughties, it even had a CD drive, and you had to dial up the internet," Margaret said, reminiscing.

"Sounds like it belongs in a museum, not a start-up," I said sarcastically.

"John said the girl at reception had trays filled with papers all over her desk. She had her headphones in and was totally disengaged. She was watching something on YouTube on her phone whilst throwing papers into the draws of a heavy silver pre-war filing cabinet that was behind the reception desk."

"So I take it they don't operate a paperless office? Interesting."

"Clearly not," Margaret said with a shake of her head. "John then asked if he could have a copy of the Wi-Fi password as he couldn't get 4G. He was curtly told, 'No' and that they've been told never to hand out their Wi-Fi password."

"How did John handle the receptionist?" I asked, amused at the unfolding of events.

"John said he became rapidly exasperated and asked to see Hans. The stroppy receptionist begrudgingly led him down a depressing brown corridor to Hans' office."

I was amazed at the contradiction from last night's event. "What was Hans like?"

"John quickly introduced himself, telling Hans he'd been online and was very impressed with his industrial pollution and wastewater filter, which was hugely successful in eliminating toxic waste. He said he needed a filter to attach to some heavy equipment that would be used in confined spaces."

"How did Hans respond?" I asked whilst refilling our coffees.

"Hans was beaming with enthusiasm. He motioned for John to take a seat in his office, which was in total disarray. Papers were lying around everywhere amongst unopened post. He noticed the calendar was three months out of date, the clock on the wall had stopped working, and the plant in the corner of his office was dead. He even had an old fax/printer rattling away on a derelict 1970s rusty table with a mint green Formica top."

"You've got to be kidding." I said. "How dare he advertise jobs for young millennials and offer them the latest and greatest? No wonder the poor girl at reception was bored. My girls don't even know what a fax is. I asked them to address an envelope the other day and gave them a stamp. They wrote the address at the top of the envelope then stuck the stamp under the address as if it was a seal at the bottom of a certificate."

Margaret smirked and said, "That's really funny."

"What else did John say?"

"Apparently, Hans was absolutely charming and proudly went into minute detail about the benefits of his technology, which he'd developed and manufactured himself. He said his latest model included remote access technology, a slick dashboard, with multi-filtration efficiency reading and the all-important toxic footprint calculator for sustainability reporting."

"Did John believe him?" I asked.

"No, not at all," Margaret said, shaking her head. "John said it didn't matter what Hans said about his technology or how great it may have been. He couldn't get beyond the deception on the website and the state of his office. There was a galaxy of difference between what he said and what John saw. It's abundantly clear you can't develop cutting edge technology and state of the art systems on a 2000's computer and software. Also, Hans' poor receptionist had to work under the most archaic conditions, in an office that wouldn't pass a health and safety inspection. He goes out of his way to recruit highly educated uni graduates, then expects them to use extinct equipment and do tedious jobs such as filing all day long."

"Unbelievable," I said. "What a revolting place to work. Good thing they do the spot-checks before giving out awards."

"Exactly," Margaret nodded. "Imagine if he'd won the award and advertised the fact on his website. It would instantly devalue the award. You only need one person to go to his place of business and then post true photos on social media."

"Or go onto Glassdoor and give a review," I said.

Listening to Margaret drove home the importance of being aware of and observing environmental and nonverbal cues. Trust can only be established when verbal and nonverbal communication are congruent.

The rest of the morning flew by. I listened to some exceptional speakers discussing the latest innovation in technology, remarkable integrated software packages for multi-destination visas, proposed changes to legislation and the effects of remote working on global mobility.

By lunch, I needed to get some fresh air to clear my head. I'd been bombarded with so much new information it felt like system overload. If I were a computer, the coloured wheel of death would be spinning!

To be perfectly honest, I was feeling quite anxious and depressed about Hans. I hadn't appreciated how easy it was to be conned and manipulated. Were people that desperate to make a quick buck they'd exploit the most vulnerable in society?

The more I learnt about the lessons in the diary, the scarier the world became.

I found a lovely spot in the park across the road from the conference centre to relax and enjoy my latte in peace. I sat amongst the most beautiful assortment of pink, white and purple winter cyclamen. Despite the grey sky, I managed to pull myself together and rang Ruben.

He asked if everything was OK. I think he could hear the frustration and weariness in my voice. I told him I didn't have much time, as I was about to give my keynote address on Cross-Fertilisation of Skills in a Multi-Generational Workforce.

I quickly summarised what I remembered from Mrs Bokman and the third principle of the diary on—Interaction.

I told him, "We're all susceptible to the laws of human nature, just like the laws of gravity. When we interact with others, we're affected by nature's pull and push. We're sensitive to people's emotions and moods, and humans tend to behave in predictable ways. There's loads of principles about interacting with others, but the main ones to be aware of are reciprocity, likability, authority, congruency, and"—I paused, losing track of my list for a moment—"the other one? Ah yes, that's right—crowd psychology."

I also explained that the whole thing was getting me down. I felt I was sinking into an abyss of endless lies, deceit and manipulation. I wasn't sure if I had the energy or desire to keep going. On top of that, I had no idea what to do next.

Ruben replied with his usual sensitivity and familiar, reassuring tone.

"Let me know what I can do to help," he said. "I prom-ised you years ago I would always be there for you. I still mean it."

I felt a tear roll down my cheek, and my heart begin to race. I hadn't had this much support and love since Arthur passed away.

Unsure of how to handle the situation. I quickly changed the subject.

I promised Ruben I'd send a copy of Mrs Bokman's notes and told him I'd finally opened her gift.

"What was it?" Ruben asked impatiently.

"She gave me a beautiful locket with a picture of my grandparents and mother as a baby. And she also gave me a note." I paused to take said note out of my bag, and read it to Ruben:

Your grandparents gave me this treasured locket when we left the camp, as a thank you. They knew I was very fond of your mother and would miss her dearly. As I'm reaching the sunset of my life, I sense it should now go to you and your daughters.

I believe an apple never falls far from the tree. I trust with all my heart that you honestly want good in the world, like your grandparents.

When two become one, the answer will be revealed. Look with your heart, and you will find the next section of the diary.

All my love

Tina xx

Ruben was silent for quite a while, taking it all in.

"Do you have any idea what two things could become one?" he asked curiously.

"No, not a clue," I said.

"Can you send me everything, including the note and a photo of the locket from all angles?" he said.

"Of course," I replied. I glanced at my watch and realised I was late. I said a brief goodbye, and hung up the phone, running back to the conference centre, as the sun was finally breaking through the clouds.

CHAPTER 9

Miranda looked absolutely beautiful. It seems like she transformed from my bubbly baby to a vivacious young lady. If only Arthur could see the girls now. He'd be so proud of his baby bears. Why did life have to be so cruel?

When we arrived, we bumped into Donna and Poppy, who were also trying to find their tickets.

We started chatting straight away, admiring each other's dresses. Donna was wearing a breathtaking, long red chiffon dress, with a scalloped neckline, pinched at the waist, emphasising her flattering figure. Poppy wore a very elegant black cocktail dress with the slightest silver thread.

"Where did you get your strapless dress?" Donna asked, gesturing to my outfit. "I love it. Very Audrey Hepburn in *Sabrina*. The delicate white satin fabric works well with your blue eyes, and the black embroidery in the bodice and full skirt give it a very regal appearance."

"Oh, this old thing, I just pulled it out of the loft," I said with a twinkle in my eye. Thank you, Harrods!

The girls no sooner got inside before they took off to the bathroom to fix their makeup. We headed straight to the board to check our table's location and to see who else would be joining us.

"Oh no, why, why did they have to do that?" I squealed.

"What's wrong?" Donna asked, leaning over me to see the table plan.

"Magda Kowalski, 'The Bitch', is sitting next to me." Right at that moment, Magda came strutting towards me in a little black dress that was clearly three sizes too small. There was no doubt she wanted everyone to admire her ample assets. She must be in her 50s by now, but with all that Botox, it's hard to tell. I don't think her face has moved since 2015.

"Hello darrrlingg!" she shrieked loudly, which made everyone turn around.

"Too late, she's seen us," I whispered to Donna.

Magda is one of those frightfully annoying people who will dominate and take over no matter what the conversation entails. She doesn't hesitate to cut people off, finish their sentence and brusquely share her bigger, louder and more dramatic story. She bulldozes her way into every conversation, no matter if it's in a group or an intimate couple.

Right on cue, "Anal Alan" arrived and discovered he's also sitting at our table.

Donna and I quickly slipped away, leaving Alan with Magda. Those two can't stand the sight of each other. She can't stand his constant nit-picking, brazen correcting and endless advice-giving. He finds her constant interruptions and the fact that her mouth rarely shuts intolerable.

We couldn't stop giggling as we headed to the ballroom, where we got a much-needed glass of champagne.

I was mesmerised by the dazzling décor in the ballroom. The organisers had clearly stepped it up a level this year.

The ballroom had been converted into a winter wonderland. It had white trees with fairy lights strategically placed throughout the room. All the tables had Nordic silver deer with candles in their antlers. A mammoth champagne fountain was the centrepiece of the room. No expense seemed to be spared—an artist had even painted the windows to resemble looking out over the Alps.

Donna and I were captivated by the creativity. We noticed the waiters were entertainers dressed as white statutes. They were motionless and suddenly changed position and topped up our glass. It freaked me out at first, but I became intrigued, trying to work out what famous statue they resembled.

Donna and I didn't see much of the girls the whole evening, except when taking selfies.

Shortly after the first course, Clementine, one of the conference organisers, asked to have a word. She's a delightful young girl of twenty-six years. Tall, and natural beauty, with delicate features and long raven hair. Her minimal makeup makes her look younger than she is but portrays freshness and sincerity. She's only been in the role for three months and is petrified of making a mistake. She's aware she's still in her probation period and wants to make a great impression. The frown on her face revealed a deep concern.

"Hi Clementine," I said with a smile. "Is everything OK? You look extremely worried."

"No, Iris, it's not." The poor girl looked quite upset. "I don't know what I'm supposed to do."

"What's wrong?" I asked, guiding her to a spot in the far corner where we could be alone.

"Two guests at Table One are being rude and loud," Clementine whispered. "They've had quite a bit to drink and have started arguing about how we judge the applications. They keep demanding I tell them who has won and insist we present the awards now."

Trying to remember what I heard about listening and asking questions, I asked, "What do you think might be the best solution?"

"I'm … I'm not sure. That's why I'm asking you," Clementine stammered.

"If you were them, what do you think you'd want?"

"To find out more information."

"Exactly. What do you think you could do?"

"I could tell them the awards will be presented straight after dinner?"

"What else could you do?" I said, giving her a reassuring look.

"I could tell them a bit about how we judge," Clementine suggested more confidently.

"Go on," I said. "How would you do that?"

"I could go on stage and make an announcement to everyone while they're eating their dinner and give a summary of how we judge the applications and why we do it that way," Clementine said, smiling proudly.

"That sounds like a very good solution to me," I said, returning her smile.

Ten minutes later, Clementine was on stage, explaining the judging process and reminding everyone about the evening's agenda. She received a loud round of applause and winked at me as she left the stage.

The awards presentation went remarkably well, despite a few disappointed applicants. Miranda rose to the occasion, smiling and shaking hands while presenting the awards and certificates.

Once her part was complete, Miranda and Poppy introduced us to their new friends Emilio and Joshua, then spent the rest of the evening on the dance floor.

By 9:45 p.m., I finally managed to have a few moments to reflect on the day. Donna was sitting at another table, catching up with friends. I sat quietly watching the world around me. I could see but not hear Alan and Magda deep in conversation. She was leaning forward, encroaching on his personal space with a disapproving look on her face. He was leaning back in his chair, arms crossed, looking down and then pointing his index figure at her trying to make a point. It did not seem to be going well.

Next to them sat Lavinia and Meredith. They worked at the same firm and got along famously. They were mimicking each other's body language and laughing in unison. When Lavinia picked up a glass of wine, Meredith followed. If Meredith put her elbow on the table, Lavinia changed position to do the same. They seemed oblivious to what they were doing.

I realised that reading nonverbal cues wasn't that difficult after all.

Sitting next to me within earshot was Joyce and Janelle. They'd never met before and were making idle conversation. It started slowly and cautiously, first revealing their names, job titles and where they worked. As Joyce began to relax, she told a little more about herself and her family, then Janelle reciprocated with the same amount of detail. They seemed to reflect each other perfectly. Joyce gave Janelle her card, and Janelle quickly followed by giving hers. Janelle filled Joyce's glass with water, and Joyce later returned the favour and filled her glass of wine. The entire conversation and body language all seemed quite unconscious and reciprocal.

I was beginning to understand more about the Law of Reciprocity. However, I was also feeling a bit confused. Luckily at that moment, Donna came back and sat next to me.

"Donna, do you know anything about reciprocity?" I asked.

"Yes, why? she said, amused.

"I get the fact that we reciprocate other people's actions, and this appears when we like the person, and we are in synch. But can an action incur a debt and make you feel guilty?" I asked.

"What do you mean?" Donna asked, raising an eyebrow.

"I have a neighbour who I hardly know. Just before Christmas, she gave me a Christmas card and an expensive bottle of wine. I was only going to give her a card. Now I feel indebted to buy her an equally expensive bottle of wine."

"Reciprocity is one of the laws of human nature," Donna replied. "We tend to feel obligated to give as we receive and to return gifts, favours and invitations. It's used a lot by marketing companies."

"In what way? I asked.

"Have you ever been to a trade show?"

"Too many to remember," I replied with a smile.

"Did you notice how companies are constantly giving away cups, pens, and novelty items?"

"Yes, I have a cupboard full of cups."

"The cups and pens aren't just for you to advertise their product, it's so you hand over your business card, and we all know what that can lead to. Endless sales calls and spam emails. By increasing the value of what is given away, the feeling of obligation to reciprocate and purchase an item will increase."

"Gosh, I'd never looked at it that way. It makes a lot of sense, though," I said, considering all the times I had received gifts.

I was fascinated by how important the laws of human nature were—how we're constantly being taken advantage of by not being aware of these principles. I felt I'd come a long way today.

On top of that, I was pleased I hadn't given Clementine a quick solution to her cries for help, which I would normally have done. This usually only resulted in the usual barrage of excuses such as:

"But I can't..."

"That's not possible..."

"It's not worth it; he won't listen anyway..."

Allowing Clementine to come up with her own solution meant that she owned it, embraced it, and positively glowed with pride when it all worked in her favour. I felt so proud of her, and at the same time, I felt like the Wise One, an actual Yoda in the making.

I felt a most successful night had finally come to a close—time to drag a very reluctant Miranda off the dance floor. Suddenly 'The Wise One' was the worst mother in the world and came crashing back down to earth.

CHAPTER 10

I arrived at the office by 10 a.m. and found most people feeling fragile and operating on their last reserves. For some it was a complete 'no show', others took a long lunch with no return. I managed to take 'clock watching' to a whole new level. At 5:30 p.m. on the dot, I shut up shop and headed home. My commute home was spent creating the usual weekend 'To-do List'. I still hadn't gotten back to Ruben, nor had I sent him Mrs Bokman's notes or photos of the locket. I decided to ask the girls to take the photos as they take a million a day and are much better than me.

As I walked through the front door, I called out to the girls, "Miranda, Melody, can you come here, please?"

"Just a sec," I heard them reply.

Miranda came bounding down the stairs, phone in hand. "Yep, what?"

"Where's Melody?" I asked.

"She's in the kitchen operating on Lulu, the fish," Miranda said without missing a beat.

"Sorry, what?" I said, not sure if I heard right.

"You know Lulu, the goldfish with the lump on his side that looks like a cauliflower? Melody's been researching the lump. Apparently, it's painless, so she decided to get rid of it before it gets bigger and kills her," Miranda, said matter-of-factly.

As I walked into the kitchen, I found Melody standing over a Starbucks cup with a Stanley knife in hand. She'd parked the fish in water with a half-cut cup placed inside the cup to keep Lulu in place. She also had her phone on a tripod filming the whole procedure.

"What are you doing?" I asked, concerned for the poor fish. I tried not to gasp at the sight.

"I'm removing Lulu's lump. Don't worry," Melody said calmly. "I've been practising on the cauliflower I found in the fridge. I first tried to tie fishing line around it and yank it off, but that didn't work. So, I'm heading straight in with the Stanley knife."

"Melody's filming a 'How to' video for YouTube," Miranda explained. "She thinks it will go viral, and she'll be an overnight sensation."

Just then, the Stanley knife slipped and nearly took out poor Lulu's eye.

"Maybe you could give Lulu a break and help me take some photos," I said, becoming increasingly concerned for Lulu.

"Sorry Mum, can't mid-operation, that's just mean."

That's what she thinks is mean! I thought. Oh my!

"Well then, Miranda, can you help me? You're such an expert at taking photos," I said.

"Sure, what do you want me to do?" Miranda replied.

I gave her the locket from Mrs Bokman and briefly explained where I got it. I showed her the lovely photo of her great grandparents and her grandmother.

"You know, we've already got one of these," Miranda said as she turned over the locket.

"What do you mean?" I asked, confused.

"I was rummaging through your jewellery box the other day looking to accessorize my new denim dress and found one almost exactly the same," she said.

"You didn't ask me if you could borrow some jewellery," I said, annoyed.

"You weren't here, and what's the point? You clearly don't know what you've got anyway."

"Can you get the locket and show me?" I asked taking a very deep breath.

"Yep, just a sec," Miranda said as she went upstairs.

Within minutes, Miranda proudly held out the locket I'd completely forgotten I owned. My mother had given it to me for my 18th birthday. I'd never really worn it. I thought it was a bit too frumpy and old fashioned.

"Excellent, thanks." I took the locket. "Can you take a few photos of the locket I received from Mrs Bokman? Let me know when you're finished. I need to unload the washing machine and return a call from my accountant about my tax return."

"Yep, no worries," she said.

When I returned from my tasks, Miranda was playing with the lockets. "You know these lockets clip together when you open them up?" she said smugly.

"That's interesting," I said, not exactly paying attention. I was reading a message from Donna.

"Look at this, Mum," Miranda called out. "When you turn them over, the squiggles on the back of each locket join to make the sign of a Leo. Just like my star sign. I'm a Leo, aren't I?"

"Yes, you are," I said. I looked up from my phone and moved over to my daughter. "Let me see that."

"No, not yet," Miranda snatched the lockets back and carefully inspected them. "Who is Leo Schmidt?" she asked, tilting her head to the side, trying to read the back of the joined lockets.

"I don't know. Where did you find the name, Leo Schmidt?" I said, leaning in, trying to see what she was reading.

"Look, when you put the lockets together, under the star sign of Leo, it says Leo Schmidt," Miranda said proudly, holding out the lockets to me.

"He's probably the man who made them. Just like an artist, the jeweller probably stamps his name in the gold," I explained. "Can you please take a photo so I can send it to Ruben? Here's my phone."

"Rightio," Miranda said, rolling her eyes and taking my phone.

After dinner, while the girls did their homework and Lulu was safely back in the tank with her lump still attached—the operation did not appear to be a success—I got back in touch with Ruben.

From: Iris
To: Ruben
Time: 8:15 p.m.
    Hey Rubes,
    Sorry it's manic. Here are the notes and some photos of the locket.
    Miranda discovered I have a similar locket. We've taken some photos of both. She also found they clip together when you turn them over, the lockets make a Leo star sign, and it looks like some guy called Leo Schmidt stamped his name on the back.
    Chat soon
    I xx

From: Ruben
To: Iris
Time: 9:00 p.m.
    Hi Rissy,
    We need to chat—I had a breakthrough.
    OK to chat now?
    R xx

I immediately picked up my phone. "Ruben, you are a genius," I said. "I can't believe I didn't put it all together and crack the code. It was staring me in the face the whole time."

"I know," Ruben said, feeling pretty chuffed with himself. "Mrs Bokman's note said: *When two become one, the answer will be revealed.*"

"It must be the two lockets which reveal the name, Leo Schmidt. But who is Leo Schmidt?" I asked.

"This is the interesting part," Ruben continued. "I went back over David Solomon's notes. Remember, some things didn't make sense. One of the quotes was: '*Observe the fourth door to the Lion's Den.*' I think that means that the fourth section has something to do with Leo Schmidt. I just got off the phone with Isaac. I asked him if he's ever heard of a man called Leo Schmidt."

"And what did he say?" I pressed, feeling increasingly impatient.

"Isaac said, when he first started working for Mr Solomon, they had a quality control manager called Leo Schmidt. He said he left way back in the 1980s and he's not even sure he's still alive. I thanked Isaac and instantly started searching through the internet."

"Go on."

"Patience! So, I found three Leo Schmidt's on LinkedIn and sent them all a quick message. I asked if any were related to the Leo Schmidt who used to work for Solomon Steel in quality control back in the 1970s. You won't believe it—within ten minutes, I got a reply."

"You're kidding!" I gasped, seriously impressed with Ruben's tenacity.

"A Leo Schmidt in Switzerland said his grandfather, also Leo Schmidt, used to work at Solomon Steel," Ruben said. "He asked if there was there something of concern. I asked if I could call him, thinking it would be a lot easier and I could sound him out."

"When are you going to speak to him?" I was so excited—we were close to finding the fourth principle.

"I just got off the phone with him. What a great guy."

"So, what happened" I asked.

"Well, this is where it gets even more interesting. I asked whether Leo's grandfather was ever in a transit camp in Holland during the war. He said he was and that he and his grandmother often spoke about the wonderful people they had met there. Then I asked if he'd ever heard about a secret diary written during that time?"

"So, what did he say?"

"He said yes—he knew quite a lot."

"Fabulous," I said, starting to feel more relieved and excited at the same time. "What do we need to do now?"

"Leo said he'd be delighted to meet and discuss what he knows," Ruben replied. "He's in Davos this weekend at a convention. We're welcome to meet him tomorrow night after the convention. Fancy a quick trip to Davos?" he asked, half-joking. "I've checked out lastminute.com. We can get cheap flights tomorrow arriving in Zurich around 2 p.m. I could meet you at Zurich airport we could then take the alpine express through the mountains to Davos. We'd be there by about 4:30 p.m."

"Where would we stay?" I asked.

"Because of the convention, accommodation in Davos is quite full, but I discovered we could get a great deal in a Wellbeing Spa hotel in St Moritz." Ruben paused. "What do you think?" He appeared, quite suddenly, reticent.

"Well… wow, it's a lot of information to take in," I replied, unsure of what to do. "How long will we be gone for?"

"I think we should come back Monday night. I know I have some annual leave and can take Monday off. What about you?"

"Um, I'm not sure. I'd have to speak to the girls and check my work diary."

"Come on, Rissy, what happened to the most spontaneous girl in the world that I used to know? You never missed an opportunity to go on an adventure. You can't give up on the diary now. We've come so far. I'm certain your grandparents would love it if you continued their mission."

"Let me think about it," I said. "I'll call you back in fifteen minutes once I've spoken to the girls."

I spoke to the girls and they were more than happy to spend the weekend at April's. Melody and April had already planned to go shopping, and Miranda had just said yes to Emilio's invite to catch a movie and pizza.

"Who's Emilio?" I asked.

"You remember the guy I introduced you to last night?" Miranda said, frustrated at my lack of recollection.

"Oh yes, which one was he, the tall one or the short one?" I asked, trying to make up for my faux pas.

"The good looking tall one," she replied, rolling her eyes, annoyed to be asked so many questions.

With the girls sorted, the only thing left was to check my diary for Monday. Back-to-back meetings. Perfect, I can just get the notes. I'm not required to make a presentation, even better.

I rang Ruben back, delighted to tell him I'd go.

He was so happy. He said, "This one's on me. I think it's time I made up for the wreck Toyota Corolla I sold you when we were twenty years old that broke down two days after you bought it."

"I remember that. It cost me a fortune to replace the clutch and brake pads," I said. "I'm happy with that."

Ruben sent me the link to my tickets an hour later. Happy days.

CHAPTER 11

The flight from London to Zurich was pleasant. I tried desperately to read the book I'd started six months ago but couldn't settle into it. Instead, I tried to remember everything I learnt from the diary. I didn't have much luck there either. My head seemed to be racing around from thought to thought. Last week had been nothing short of crazy at work. I decided it would be better to speak to Ruben on the train to Davos about the diary.

Touching down in Zurich instantly lightened my mood. The weather was stunning, with clear blue skies, a slight breeze and snow-capped mountains as far as the eyes could see. I'd been dreaming of crunching through fresh snow in the Alps for the past week.

Heading down the escalators to the train station below the airport, I had my fingers crossed Ruben's flight was on time. I would be seriously unimpressed if I ended up on another train by myself.

To my delight, not only was Ruben waiting in the café, but a vanilla latte and slice of banana loaf were also waiting. Timed to perfection, thirty minutes later, we were on the train to Davos with a table seat, phone sockets and a huge window to enjoy the view of the mountains.

I felt slightly disappointed that there was barely any snow in Zurich, just a few patches here and there. We had a fluttering of snowing as we left the station, but it wasn't settling on the ground, just some slush. I'd heard the last few days had been mild. I hope it's better in the mountains. It would be such a shame to have mucky slush. I get enough of that in London, I thought dismally.

Ruben and I spent the first half hour of our journey catching up on gossip whilst taking in the city architecture.

"How are Sarah and the kids?" I asked. "Enjoying their summer holidays?"

"I've hardly had a chance to speak to them," he said. "It's hard with the time difference between Holland and Australia. The school holidays don't help. They're always catching up with friends, going to the beach, and Sarah's been buying new school uniforms, shoes, books etc." He pulled himself away from the view from the window and asked me, "How are your girls?"

"Good, Melody decided to operate on Lulu, the fish—don't ask! The fish is somehow still alive. Miranda is going on a date with a boy she met at the awards night. I'm suddenly very aware of how quickly time is passing us by."

"Speaking of time, have you had much time to think about the diary?" Ruben enquired.

"I've tried," I confessed, "but there's just so much to take in. I'm not sure where to start."

"Let's go back over what we know," Ruben suggested, the cogs of his methodical mind turning. "Isaac said we're going through the Fourth Industrial Revolution, also known as the Digital Revolution, which has significantly changed the way we communicate."

"Well, yes, that's certainly true," I said. "The girls don't socialise with their friends the way we used to. We couldn't wait to get out of the house and meet at the park or at each other's house. They're always on their phone, sending messages, selfies and videos rather than meeting in person."

"My kids are the same," Ruben confessed. "But now they use voice activation instead of typing." He paused and continued, "I was reading all the sections we've seen so far and believe there must be a reason why they put them in a certain order. One principle seems to build on the other."

I nodded, and Ruben carried on: "David Solomon's notes indicate that 'Awareness' is the first principle of the diary. Awareness is not only about ourselves, and others; it's also about the environment and all nonverbal cues. By increasing our awareness, we realise there's a lot more going on deep beneath the surface of our superficial conversations. We become conscious of listening between the lines and recognising the implicit and explicit messages. All communication conveys several messages simultaneously. Words carry the explicit message, how the listener feels, and his thoughts are the implicit message."

"That's very true," I said. "I've noticed over the past week, as my awareness increased, my conversations have increased exponentially in meaning and purpose."

"If you think about it, 'Awareness' is the key to the next principle of 'Empathy'. Without awareness, there can be no empathy. People receive communication through their filters," Ruben said.

"I totally agree," I said. "It's very true—it's not what you say, it's what people hear. People won't remember your words; they'll remember how you made them feel. Anyone who's dealt with kids will agree."

"You could say, 'Awareness' opens the door to conscious communication and empathy," Ruben suggested. "This then leads to the third principle, 'Interaction'. There can be no communication without interaction. Understanding the laws of human nature unveils a new view of life. When you open up to the laws of reciprocity, likability, authority, congruency and crowd psychology, you begin to communicate wholistically, using your whole mind, whole body and whole system, which in turn reveals a whole new level of understanding."

I was listening intently. "It's so simple and makes a lot of sense when you summarise it like that," I said thoughtfully. "Do you think the last two principles are that simple?"

"I hope so," Ruben muttered, clearly deep in thought.

We sat quietly for quite some time, totally consumed in our thoughts, and the stunning scenery gently unfolded around us. We'd left Zurich by now, and we were heading into the mountains. The view had changed entirely. Snow was now falling heavily and settling on the endless fields with scattered steep-roofed farmhouses. The train meandered around tight bends and sheer rock face mountains steaming through deep valleys and charming villages with medieval churches.

Ruben broke our silence by gently asking, "Rissy, I hope you don't mind me asking, I've been wanting to for years but never had the right opportunity. Please tell me if I'm prying—I won't mind if you don't feel comfortable."

"It's OK," I said. "We've always been completely honest with each other. I don't have anything to hide. What would you like to know?"

"I was in complete shock when I heard what happened to Arthur. I can't explain the pain I felt for you, for your loss and sorrow. I only heard bits from my parents, who'd heard bits from your parents. But I never heard what actually happened. Only that he died suddenly. What happened?" he asked softly with genuine concern and kindness.

I took a deep breath. I started slowly, reluctantly, not wanting to relive the pain.

"As you know, Arthur and I got married when I was very young, only twenty-one years old. I had absolutely no doubts about marrying him. From the day we met, our relationship seemed to flow. We were in total harmony with each other. Time passed so quickly when we were together. That didn't mean we didn't fight. Of course, we did. He was also a lawyer. Have you ever met a lawyer who wasn't determined to win an argument and have the last word?"

"However, our arguments were inspiring, and we learnt a lot from each other. I poured all my trust and love into our relationship. The day before he died, we'd taken the girls to friend's birthday party. They were laughing and playing without a care in the world. I remember pinching myself, thinking how lucky I was to have my perfect little family, a fantastic job and to be living in the most beautiful part of the world. I felt totally blessed.

The very next morning, in the blink of an eye, my entire world shattered. Two police officers knocked on my door and told me Arthur had fallen from our balcony, from the 20th floor. There are no words to describe the depth of my pain and despair. I kept thinking I would wake up from this horrible nightmare, but every morning I had a haunting realisation my world had been ripped apart forever."

"I'm so sorry, Rissy," Ruben said with sadness in his eyes. "I never realised how traumatic it must have been for you."

"I'm not sure if you knew Arthur suffered from depression," I continued, trying not to tear up. "Back then, mental health wasn't talked about like it is today. He was embarrassed and ashamed that someone of his mental capacity and intelligence could have a mental disorder. He spoke to a specialist in mental health, but unfortunately, he couldn't connect to the therapist and stopped going. He felt lost in his darkness and couldn't find a way out.

"After his death, I decided I would have to become both Mum and Dad. I strapped on my fighting harness and built a wall around myself. It is true; we do more to avoid pain than gain pleasure."

"What do you mean?" Ruben asked, concerned.

"Like this train journey, life is full of twists and turns. There are many blind corners where you have no clue what's coming next. I went through a period of 'obnoxious behaviour' after Arthur's death. I became fiercely independent, totally self-sufficient and determined to stay completely in control. I felt the only person I could trust was myself. I became very strong but at the cost of being self-absorbed. I lost touch with the concerns of others. I became isolated from the world around me and consumed in my own drama."

"Is that why I hadn't heard from you for so many years," Ruben realised sorrowfully.

"Yes, the fear of ever being hurt again meant my communication and subsequent relationships had no depth," I nodded. "I guarded my thoughts and feelings with the same ferocity as security guards at a Swiss bank vault. The laws of human nature are very accurate. As I became a closed book, others would reciprocate and be a closed book as well."

"I hadn't realised you'd shut out people to that extent. How did you cope?" Ruben asked, with sadness in his eyes.

"I threw myself into my work and focussed on the girls. I now understand, as I've travelled through life, whenever I got near a tunnel, I'd jump off the train. I couldn't stand the darkness of the unknown. I watched others continue on their journey to happiness. They had the courage to proceed through the unfamiliar tunnel. Somehow, I'd subconsciously lost my courage amongst the graveyard of buried hopes and dreams when I lost Arthur."

"Do you think the diary has changed your thoughts and ideas about communication?" Ruben asked, deeply worried about my welfare.

"Absolutely," I nodded, "I think the diary has prised opened my world. I'm now aware of myself and what I did to cope. I'm also aware of how others perceive me. It's lifted a veil, allowing me to see the world through the eyes of others."

"I'm happy for you, Rissy, and I'm sure your grandparents would be very happy for you too. I've found the principle on empathy is extremely powerful, especially from an emotional perspective," Ruben shared.

"I agree, becoming aware has allowed me to reconnect with my own emotions, which has subsequently given me the ability to empathise with others and understand their emotions. I realised this the other night when I stopped myself from solving Clementine's dilemma. Taking the time to understand her and her concerns, listening and asking relevant questions so Clementine could solve her own problem filled me with a new understanding, empathy and resulting joy," I said, then asked, "Have you learnt anything new from the third principle of interaction?"

"Yes, I've found I'm more conscious when I interact with others," Ruben replied. "Before communicating, I stop myself from going on autopilot. I take a few moments to assess the environment and all the surrounding nonverbal cues. I make sure I'm completely present in mind and body. I also stop and consider my emotions and whether I'm in sync with the other person."

"There is so much to learn, isn't there? Do you think we need to do more research into the principles of the diary?"

"I don't think so," Ruben nodded. "They've made the principles very simple to follow. Anyway, being knowledgeable is no replacement for experience. Knowledge means absolutely nothing if you don't use it. The law of congruency is a perfect example. I'm very guilty of 'Do as I say, not as I do'. I'd never realised how it causes the opposite of what you're trying to achieve. You simply create mistrust and loss in faith."

Just at that moment, and without even realising it, our train had gone through a very long, dark tunnel. The daylight revealed a magical snow-covered hamlet. The train slowed down, allowing us to take in the majestic dark-wood chalets with ornate curlicued designs. We were mesmerised by the deep green forest and looming mountains. The following fifteen minutes, we spent in silence transfixed by a succession of charming villages with the hallmarks of a Hans Christian Andersen fairy tale.

Approaching St Moritz, we were greeted by old-world glamour. It felt like we'd stepped back in time and entered a 1950s Hollywood film set.

"Do you realise," Ruben said proudly, "that Switzerland has remained neutral and has not fought in any international war since 1815. They were neutral in both World War One and Two."

"I had no idea," I said, impressed with his knowledge.

"They must understand the basic principles of communication," Ruben continued. "Instead of fighting in wars,

Switzerland has frequently been involved in peace-building negotiations around the world."

As we got off the train, my thoughts refocussed on finding the next section of the diary.

"I can't wait to hear what Leo Schmidt says about the fourth section." I said, gathering all my bags and leaving the train.

CHAPTER 12

T he taxi from the station to the hotel only took five minutes through a few side streets and up a very steep hill. When we arrived, I was in a state of shock.

"Ruben, what is this?" I asked. "Are you out of your mind?" I wasn't sure whether to be annoyed or cry with joy. "You do realise the wreck you sold me was a Toyota, not a Rolls Royce."

"I know, Rissy, but we had so many wild and wonderful dreams together, and we never managed to fulfil one. I thought I'd make up for it," Ruben said, smiling proudly.

"By combining all our dreams into one mega dream?" I queried.

"That's one way of looking at it."

In front of us was not a 'Wellbeing Centre' but rather Badrutt's Palace Hotel with a Wellness Spa.

"I watched a *Lifestyles of the Rich and Famous* TV programme which showcased this hotel," I said, astonished at the grandeur of the hotel. "Movie stars, rock stars, models, Formula One drivers, royalty and even Instagrammers love to stay here." I turned around, taking in the view.

"I know," Ruben said, "but you're worth it! You've been through so much and have struggled for so long. It's about time you let someone do something nice for you."

A gracious doorman in a military-style, grey woollen overcoat and burgundy hat opened the heavy wooden door. The foyer led to a casual dining area with wood panelling, red velvet chairs and an enormous floor to ceiling dome-shaped window looking out over the lake and mountains.

"Do we have time for a quick drink before heading to Davos?" I asked, desperate to take in more of the view.

"Unfortunately not, but we've got all of tomorrow and Monday morning," Ruben affirmed.

The bellboy showed us to our adjoining rooms and quickly gave us a tour of the wellbeing centre and pool.

Precisely two hours later, we were in Davos at the convention centre meeting Leo Schmidt Jr. Davos is more of a business centre in the Alps compared to St Moritz, which is old-world charm and glamour.

We instantly recognised Leo from his LinkedIn profile as he approached us at the reception desk. I thought Ruben was tall, but Leo towered over him with his slim frame. He had thinning hair and smart business glasses. At a guess, I'd say he was in his late 50s. He wore what looked like a dated but comfortable business suit.

Leo was perfectly on time, had the most immaculate manners and was highly proficient in English. After the introductory pleasantries, he suggested we go to a small restaurant in the village where it would be quieter.

The restaurant was an adorable traditional Swiss-style chalet in the centre of Davos. We thanked Leo for taking the time out of his busy schedule to talk to us about what he knew about the diary. Without going into all the details, I explained my grandparents had been in the transit camp, and we were trying to find the sections of the lost diary.

Leo was very open and willing to help. He'd heard his parents talk about my grandparents and felt his parents would be thrilled for him to help us in our quest.

Leo explained his grandparents were both young and recently married when they were taken from their home in Germany and placed in the transit camp in Westerbork. They'd been detained with both of their parents and several other people they knew. Tragically over two years, they slowly lost both sets of parents and most of their friends due to being placed on trains to termination camps.

"I believe you have two lockets made by my grandfather whilst he was in the camp," Leo inquired. "My grandfather was a gifted man and a master craftsman. He came from a long line of jewellers and watchmakers. Do you have the lockets with you?"

"I do. Would you like to see?" I asked.

I showed him the two lockets with Leo's name, inscribed. It was clear Leo was overcome with pride as he examined the pieces.

"Did your grandfather do much work as a watchmaker or jeweller while he was in the camp?" I asked.

"Not really," Leo replied. "All the prisoners were stripped of their jewellery as soon as they entered the camp. My grandfather repaired some of the officers' and other staff members' watches. Because of his skill and expertise, my grandfather was told to sort the confiscated jewellery. That's how he found the gold he'd brought in with him and was able to make your lockets. He'd told me about them and how much joy it gave him during the camp's challenging times to be creative. He gave your grandparents the lockets as a thank you for saving their lives. One locket was for your grandmother, the other for your mother."

"Do you know how my grandparents saved your grandparents' lives?" I asked. I was thoroughly enjoying learning so much about my grandparents.

"Your grandfather had arranged for my grandparents work, which prevented them from going on the trains," Leo explained.

"What type of work did your grandparents do in the camp?" Ruben asked.

"They were fortunate to be included on the essential worker list, which prevented them from being placed on the trains to Auschwitz. My grandmother, Martha worked in the communal kitchen, and my grandfather helped build various cabins and facilities as they continually expanded the camp to accommodate more displaced Jews."

"And for how long were your grandparents in the camp?" I asked gently, trying to be sensitive.

"From September 1942 until liberation," Leo replied. "Their house and entire belongings in Germany were taken by the Nazis when detained in the camp." He paused and then said, matter-of-factly, "They were basically stripped of their entire identity."

"Did your grandparents talk much about their time in the camp?" I enquired.

"Yes, over time, and as I got older, they spoke more about it," Leo said.

"Did your grandfather ever mention the secret meetings?" Ruben asked.

"Yes, my grandfather spent a great deal of time educating me on the secret meetings and Communication Intelligence incorporating the Fourth Dimension in Communication. He was very proud of what he'd learnt. It's quite amazing that you have both lockets in your possession. It's a significant sign."

"Why is that?" I asked, confused.

"My grandfather stressed everyone had agreed to keep the information in the diary out of the public eye for fear of the contents being used negatively, as I believe you already know. They divided the diary into five parts, and every member would be the guardian of a section. Due to the enormous uncertainty at the time, they were unsure when to release the entire contents to the public."

"So, what did they do after they divided up the sections?" I asked.

"Your grandparents decided to give one of the lockets to another member who was part of the diary's creation," Leo explained. "They choose Tina, the wife of Hans Bokman Snr, the camp accountant and a truly honourable man. They believed when the lockets came together; it would be a sign that the time was approaching for the information to be released."

I was desperate to find out more about the 'sign' but didn't want to interrupt Leo.

He continued, "The friendships formed in the camp were built on their shared experiences and created a deep sense of trust. David Solomon chaired the secret meetings. He was a very successful, influential man before the war. David's business, Solomon Steel, was the leading supplier of fabricated steel to the government. After the war, he continued running his business employing many of the men he met in the transit camp. My grandfather was one of them. Mr Solomon employed my grandfather for nearly twenty-five years as his quality control manager. Sadly, my grandfather passed away ten years ago."

"Do you know why your grandfather was given the fourth section?" Ruben asked.

"Yes, while in the camp Mr Solomon was very impressed with my grandfather's immaculate attention to detail and timekeeping. The fourth section focusses on 'Observation' but not just any observation; it focusses on observing time and space."

"Do you have a copy of the fourth section?" I asked, filled with anticipation.

"Not on me." Leo shook his head. "I'll have to search through my parent's belongings to see if I can locate the original. But I can tell you what it says," he said with confidence. "As you know, awareness is the first step in communication. If awareness is the key, then observation is the doorway to improving communication."

"That sounds profound," Ruben said. "We thought each section must build on the previous. Do you know what was the basis for this section?"

"The members of the secret meetings who helped create the diary had been in contact with many famous scientists before they arrived at the camp. Viktor Frankl heavily influenced our section. He raised a very valid point that was the basis for this section," Leo clarified.

4. Observation—The fourth principle in Communication Intelligence

Viktor Frankl stated—"Between every action and response, there is a space. In that space, we have the power to choose our response.

The members took this one step further:

"Between every action and reaction, there is a space. In that space, you have the power to choose the time and response."

"As you may be aware, the Swiss are very well known for their timekeeping. It's part of our culture and one of the reasons for our success," Leo pointed out. "Time is the one commodity that everyone on the face of the planet has in equal proportion. It doesn't matter how wealthy you are, your status, education or title. It doesn't even matter what time zone you live in."

"I can relate to that," I said. "I never seem to have enough time, especially at work, when people constantly interrupt me."

"When you have disregard for other people's time, whether by keeping them waiting or wasting their time, you instantly cause a feeling of disrespect and annoyance," Leo continued. "You will also lose credibility. Have you ever tried having a conversation with someone who's running out the door or whilst they are deep in thought completing a task? Today the most common struggle is attempting to have a conversation whilst the listener is on a device. Communication is doomed to fail as there is no connection between the source and receiver. A brilliant employee will be looked over for promotion if there is a consistent pattern of being late to work, or late completing a task, as they are perceived as unreliable."

"Is that it?" I asked. "I'm confused. It seems a bit too simple."

"Would you like to go to the ice rink just down the road?" Leo suggested. "I can explain. Can you ice skate?" He had a big smile on his face.

"I've been a couple of times, but I'm not great," I said as we headed towards the ice rink. "Ruben is much better than me."

"Ice skating is the perfect example of nonverbal communication and observing time and space," Leo said, rationalising the principle.

"Tell me what you can see on the ice?" Leo asked me.

"I see a lot of people going in many different directions. Some are doing spins, some jumping, a couple trying to ice-dance, and over there I see a couple pair skating with the woman above the man's head," I said, observing the twenty people on the ice rink.

"What else can you tell me?" Leo asked.

"It's manic out there; you need eyes in the back of your head not to get sliced," I said, scared someone was about to get a blade in their leg.

"Exactly," Leo confirmed. "Awareness is a fundamental element to survival, whether on the ice or in everyday life. Skaters need to perfect not only their balance but also timing. In a practice session with many skaters of different ability, the skater has to constantly scan the environment and space available to practice a jump or move. They monitor nonverbal cues, from not only other skaters but also the state of the ice, to make sure they don't fall in a hole or trip over an object on the ice such as a leaf."

"I think you have to be just as vigilant when you visit a country for the first time," Ruben added.

"Yes, it's very similar to being in a new country. Have you noticed you have a heightened sensitivity to nonverbal cues, especially when you don't understand the language?" Leo asked us. "You pick up more sounds, smell, signs and symbols."

"How does this relate to conversations?" I asked.

"Unfortunately, people tend to go on autopilot when they jump into a conversation," Leo elaborated. "They don't stop to think about the listener of the communication. You wouldn't behave that way when you approach a busy road. You would stop, look and listen. You follow the road rules, stop at red lights and are cautious when approaching traffic. Whether you're a pedestrian, on a bike, scooter or in a car, you find the right time and space to join the traffic. You read and respect the nonverbal cues, especially time and space." Leo pointed to the traffic before us. "There is no difference with communication."

"I'm confused. Why don't people use this simple Time and Space—Stop, Look and Listen methodology when communicating? I don't understand why it should be a secret?" I asked.

"An excellent question," Leo replied. "The section on its own is harmless; it's when it's combined with the other sections, that's when it can be used negatively," he attested.

"We heard when we were in Holland there are people who are determined to keep the information in the diary suppressed. By the sounds of it, they'd rather not find the right time to release it. Have you heard this?" Ruben asked.

"Yes, there's an organisation an Intellectual Society in Holland with a Chapter in Davos which is determined to keep the information out of the public domain," Leo said.

"I still don't get it," I said. "We've learnt so much positive, useful information. Why suppress it?"

"There are three elderly members, who are amongst the last survivors of Auschwitz who had been held in transit in Westerbork. They are afraid of the consequences if the diary is released. They quite rightly feel many people have dark intentions. Many people in today's world are still very easily influenced," Leo said, concerned.

"He does have a point," I said. "I recently met a man who's had the privilege of knowing one of the sections and used it to manipulate people."

"Do you mean Hans Bokman Jr.?" Leo asked, frowning.

"Yes, I do."

"Unfortunately, Hans Jr. is one reason the elders want the diary kept from the public. We're keeping a close eye on him. The Intellectual Society was notified only the other day of his involvement with a cybersecurity issue, and we fear further cyber warfare."

Ruben and I just looked at each other. I could tell we were thinking the same thing—we were wondering if Hans Jr. was behind Ruben's computer hack.

"Leo, has anyone considered critical mass awareness or the Tipping Point Theory?" I suggested. "If enough good people learnt the principles in the diary, wouldn't they be able to influence others positively? It would seem to me if the general public were aware of manipulation methods during communication, it would lead to fewer people being manipulated."

"That's a fascinating point, Iris," Leo said with a hint of enthusiasm. "We've been having discussions recently whether there's any merit in creating a certification and training programme on the contents of the diary."

"Do you think it will go ahead?" I asked, intrigued by the concept.

"Sadly, not at the moment. The elders are very concerned about Hans Bokman Jr. Also, they've heard very worrying feedback about the effects of social media on the young and vulnerable. Someone raised the issue of personalisation and relevance on social media in the last meeting."

"What does that mean?" I asked, confused.

"Large organisations are using artificial intelligence to analyse personal data on social media sites, creating extremely in-depth, accurate profiles of the user. They then use this personal data to direct ads and newsfeeds that are highly relevant to the consumer user. These relevant feeds confirm the user's ideological beliefs, which dramatically amplify confirmation bias."

"What do you mean by confirmation bias?" Ruben asked.

"It means they feed information that conforms to the user's values and beliefs and denies a balanced view of the world," Leo explained. "Unlike in the past, everyone received the same news broadcast when watching TV or reading a paper. Now two people can sit next to each other and receive completely different news updates depending on their profile and beliefs. These organisations have already mastered the concept of time and space."

"I wasn't aware of that," I said, annoyed at being targeted by artificial intelligence. "I can appreciate why the elders would have some concerns then. But what are your thoughts, Leo?"

"I believe the world has gone through a paradigm shift in communication," Leo explained. "The pandemic has brought people from all over the world closer together. Technology such as Zoom calls have forced people to remove their mask. From one day to the next, we were transported into people's living room, kitchen or bedroom. This opened the door to greater awareness of the challenges and stresses people at work encounter at home, such as small children, elderly parents and people with disabilities. The length of the lockdown resulted in people becoming more willing to show their vulnerabilities. This, in turn, made people more empathetic towards others. People seem to have a greater appreciation of time and space. Many employers are now taking into consideration the demands of working from home, the difficulty in managing home-schooling, the various household timetables, available space to work from home, the effects of isolation, and mental health issues."

"It sounds like you think it may be the right time to make the diary's contents public," I asked.

"Maybe yes. It could be the right time to incorporate Communication Intelligence and the Fourth Dimension in Communication in our day-to-day lives. But we still have to be careful of the evil intentions of people like Hans Bokman Jr. and manipulation through artificial intelligence," Leo said cautiously.

"Do you use this information in your line of work as well?" I asked.

"I most certainly do," Leo said proudly. "But to be honest, I don't even think about it. It's like second nature, just like walking down the street. I chair a board that monitors industry standards and compliance. We provide communication platforms, forums and training. We also audit organisations around the world. Our systems flow because we respect observing the principle of time and space."

Leo looked at his watch and mentioned it was time to leave as he promised his wife he'd be home by 10 p.m. We couldn't thank him enough for all his help and insights. Just before he left, I had to ask, "Leo, do you know where I can get a copy of the last section of the diary? We are so close to putting it all together."

"I'm sorry, Iris. I made a promise to my grandfather, as he'd made to the other members that we would not reveal the name of the guardians. However, what I can say is: *'Mr Solomon held the key and supplied the infrastructure. His genius successfully mined the minds of all the members. He combined their strength and raw resources to create the new material in the diary.'* I wish you the very best. Only time will tell if you are the one to share it with the world."

Ruben and I looked at each other with excitement. We couldn't wait to go back over what we found in Mr Solomon's tin box.

CHAPTER 13

I woke to a crystal-clear morning with blues skies as far as the eye could see. Icicles were hanging off rooftops like candy canes in a sweet shop. All around were skiers heading to the many chair lifts, excited to be the first to carve up the fresh morning snow.

With every breath I inhaled of the crisp, clean mountain air, I felt a sense of peace and tranquillity. Looking down at the leafless trees reaching out over the crowds below, I suddenly remembered the dream I had last night.

I was in a faraway land in Guatemala in a small village called Momostenango. It was a serene autumn afternoon, with a light breeze sweeping lifeless leaves across my path. I stood in front of a tree adorned with hundreds of pieces of coloured fabric. I felt mesmerised by the beauty yet sadness of this enormous tree. I tied a small section of Arthur's favourite scarf with my name on it to a branch with a fork. The tree was the Tree of the Broken-Hearted. People from all over the world had travelled here to place a piece of fabric with their name inscribed to a branch. They'd watch it blow in the wind like a kite, praying in their heart they would be healed and set free. As I gazed up at the tree, I was overcome by the sudden unbounded stillness that descended on the world around me.

I then saw myself examining a picture of Leonardo da Vinci's *Last Supper*. I was contemplating the diversity of the expressive facial expressions and body language when my alarm abruptly woke me.

Remembering the dream made me feel heavy and unsettled. A state of emptiness and sadness swept over me like the autumn leaves in my dream.

Pulling myself together, I met Ruben for breakfast downstairs in the dining room of Badrutt's Palace Hotel. Breakfast was the most amazingly sumptuous and well-presented Eggs Florentine I have ever had. I'm not in the habit of taking photos of my food, but even I succumbed. Our table was in front of a vast dome window giving us breath-taking views of snow-capped mountains and the lake below. Live harp music accompanied our every bite. I wanted the moment to last forever.

Breaking my enchanted moment, Ruben announced triumphantly;

"I just found it." He was looking at David Solomon's notes: *'To steal the thoughts of others brings a new low to business and mankind.'*

"What did you find?" I asked, trying to see his notes.

"I need to speak to Isaac first thing in the morning," Ruben said proudly.

"About what?" I asked.

"As we know, every section is connected to Mr Solomon," Ruben said. "Remember what Leo Schmidt said: 'Mr Solomon held the key and supplied the infrastructure. His genius successfully mined the minds of all the members. He combined their strength and raw resources to create the new material in the diary.' I need to find out who else Mr Solomon employed around 1945, who his suppliers were, his business associates. I think it could be the missing link. I'm so excited." Ruben took the last big bite of his enormous Full English breakfast with double bacon and sausage.

"Excellent!" I replied, trying to sound enthusiastic but only interested in having a relaxing day in the mountains.

"So, what's the plan for the day?" he asked, taunting and prodding me in the ribs with the same excitement he had when we were ten years old and running out the door to build a raft and drift down the river. Life was so simple back then. We were thrilled by the undisclosed gift the day had in store. We weren't concerned about what could go wrong. We were up for all challenges. We knew full well while drifting down the river, on our self-made raft we could capsize or sink at any moment. We jumped, splashed and hurdled things at each other all day long, never insulted by the extreme measures we took to bring the other one down.

Back then, everyone thought we'd sail through life together. However, nature had other ideas, from nowhere the winds of change came along and swept us in entirely different directions. They say you meet people for a season or a reason. I wondered what the reason for us coming back together was? Could there be more than the diary?

"Hello, anyone home?" Ruben said as he took a sneaky bite off my plate.

"Sorry, the plan?" I said, coming back to reality.

"I thought we could take a walk on the lake; there are loads of people on it. It doesn't freeze every year, so it's a must. I saw a van selling sausages in the middle, so it must be safe, and apparently, there's a vintage car show starting at 10 a.m. at the northern part of the lake. After lunch, there's a polo match taking over most of the lake, so we should go sooner than later."

I surprised Ruben by reserving a table for lunch at the most sought after restaurant in St Moritz, standing at 8,000 feet in the Swiss Alps. We had to take a cable car which stopped at the base of Piz Nair. Mathis restaurant is a traditional rustic-pub style brasserie, with frill-free décor. It attracts movie stars (who advertise coffee machines), the wives of ex-presidents, retired Wimbledon champions and everything in between. We were fortunate to get a seat on the terrace after lunch with fur-lined chairs and a beaver lap blanket. We blissfully spent a couple of hours soaking up the sun whilst drinking red wine. We laughed and joked as we did on those old rafts, completely uninhibited in our bubble of unconditional love.

Back in the hotel, I tried calling the girls several times but couldn't get through. It appears communication is entirely on their terms when it comes to a device.

I decided to make the most of the wellbeing centre and had a massage followed by a swim in the infinity pool. Ruben joined me poolside after he finished watching the football.

"You know, I was thinking about Leo and the time and space section," I said whilst getting into the spa behind the waterfall flowing into the pool. "Shortly after Arthur died, I was trying to juggle being a mum and a dad, balancing work and taking care of the girls. Trust me, I did not manage my time well. I was always late picking the girls up from school. When I arrived, they were the only children left in the playground, usually walking along the top a fence to see if my car was approaching. One day the penny dropped. I decided to put myself in their shoes. I placed myself at the back gate after school, feeling abandoned, wondering if something had happened. All the other children had parents who were on time. I realised I had a choice. I could change my priorities, put the girls at the top of my list instead of finishing another call with a client before picking them up. I was never late again. I didn't have to work on changing my habits. I didn't have to set reminders. I knew they were the most important thing in my life. I also realised it was cruel to let them worry something had happened to me day after day by being late. I managed the space between my actions and reactions. It completely transformed the stress in all of our lives."

Ruben gave me his reassuring smile. Then he noticed his phone ringing.

"It's Sarah," he said. "Mind if I take this?"

"Of course not," I said.

Ruben sent a message half an hour later to say he was sorry he couldn't make dinner; Sarah and the kids asked if he could Zoom call them.

I stayed poolside, reliving the most wonderful day. A sudden wave of sadness took hold. I realised that, over the years, I've been extremely determined to control every situation. I have wonderful friends, a supportive family and a fulfilling job. I thought I had it all worked out. My routine suits me, and it works. It's predictable, it's simple, and it doesn't change. Why then did I feel a void inside? A void I had denied, a void that had grown deeper and wider the more I ignored it. Gnawing away at my soul, growing in the darkness of denial.

I finally allowed the light to penetrate through. I confessed to myself, despite my ability to weather any storm. Deep inside, I longed for love.

A knot of anxiety grew in my stomach.

What am I doing? I thought. I was happy before I started looking for the diary. Why should I look for the last section? What good can come of it? Is it worth knowing all this stuff when it just makes me more miserable?

Ping!

From: Melody
To: Iris
    Mum, you're never going to guess who Emilio is related to?
    Ha! Ha! Ha!
    Melody xxx

I had no idea this message would change everything.

CHAPTER 14

Melody still hadn't replied to my text, nor had Miranda. Obviously, they thought it was a great game to keep me in suspense.

It's incredible how quickly you leave the peace and tranquillity of a break behind before you've even left the location. My morning was spent packing, checking I hadn't left anything behind, checking emails and messages. My body may have been in the Alps, but my mind had cleared out before stepping out of bed. A wave of melancholy had replaced the merriment of the last couple of days. I noticed my conversations with Ruben had flatlined. We were both deep in thought, heading back to Zurich airport.

Standing in the queue at passport control, I decided to entertain myself by watching the passing trade. It seemed as good a time as any to work on my nonverbal communication skills.

I noticed I was starting to tap my foot impatiently while the man at the window couldn't find his passport. The colour had drained from his face; a wave of sheer desperation had taken over him. He frantically searched his back pocket, then his bag, then his laptop bag and back to his back pocket, but couldn't find it. He began arguing with the woman beside him. I didn't have to hear one word to work out what was going on. Behind him was an older woman, with purple hair, wearing Doc Martens and a long black coat which emitted a frightful stench of smoke and incense. Her unbuttoned coat revealed a t-shirt with 'Psycho Bitch' written in giant print. Her face matched her t-shirt. I instantly decided to stay clear of her.

I nudged Ruben. "Check her out," I said. Startled, he looked up from his phone. He wasn't happy; he'd been watching a football match and wasn't in the mood to check anyone out.

It dawned on me how instinctively I not only read but respond to nonverbal and environmental cues. It seems to be strongest when my mind is empty. It also helps when I'm actively focussed on the environment. Whether we're bone idle in an airport queue or focussed on a football match, we're still able to read nonverbal cues when we make an effort and concentrate. Let's face it, to me, a football match is just a nonverbal story with a bunch of men running after the same ball and hugging each other.

○ ○ ○

I couldn't wait to get home and tell the girls all about the last couple of days but decided to hold back and give them a chance to go first.

"How was your weekend, girls? Did you have much success shopping?" I asked trying to be light and sprightly.

"Yeah, good, I bought a new pink sweater," Melody said eagerly.

"How was your date with Emilio?" I asked cautiously, wondering whether to come right out and ask who he was related to.

Miranda delighted in dancing around the issue. In minute detail, she happily told me all about the movie, then slowly moved on to every bite of her sensational ham and pineapple pizza.

After twenty minutes, I finally caved. "So, I hear Emilio is related to someone I know?" I said casually.

"Oh my god, you'll never guess. Well, I'll give you three guesses," said Miranda.

"I give up," I said.

"No, you have to guess," she insisted.

"OK, Emilio Brown, Smith, Jones."

"No, that's cheating," she said.

"OK, if you don't want to tell me, that's fine," I said and walked off.

"Bokman!" she shouted as I left the room.

"What?" I said, spinning around, looking at her with astonishment.

"He's the son of that man you don't like, Hans Bokman," Melody said, grinning from ear to ear.

"Is that true?" I asked Miranda, desperately hoping it was another one of their jokes.

"Yep, that's him," she said, gloating.

Trying to keep my rage to a low simmer, I said, "I don't think it's a good idea that you continue seeing him. His father has the morals of a sewer rat."

"That's not very fair!" she snapped back with her hands on her hips. "You can't judge Emilio to be the same as his father just because you don't like him. You wouldn't want people judging you to be just like your mother. Just because Grandma was permanently in a bad mood and sour with everyone, doesn't mean people should judge you to be the same."

She does have a point, I thought. Deep breath.

"Why don't you tell me about him then," I said, turning on the kettle.

"He's eighteen and really kind and sweet. He's also very good looking," Miranda said, smiling like a Cheshire cat.

"I remember now. You introduced Emilio to me at the awards night. He is very good looking," I said, doing my best to be supportive.

"He just started uni," Miranda continued. "He's studying a combined degree in computer science and behavioural science with a major focus on human-machine interaction and decision-making. He said he wants to be an expert in intelligence interrogation."

"What does that mean?" I said, feeling totally out of my depth.

"I'm not 100% sure—he said it means something like understanding artificial intelligence systems, what they can do and their limitations," Miranda said tentatively.

"That sounds interesting," I said. "Is he enjoying it?"

"He said he loves it. He's really, really intelligent. He topped his year at school. But that doesn't mean he's a dork!" Miranda clarified.

"I'm sure he's not," I said. "Does he have any hobbies?"

"Just regular stuff. He didn't chat that much about himself. But was really interested in me. He asked lots of questions. He even asked about you?"

"Really, that's very kind of him," I said, starting to become a bit suspicious. "What did you say?"

"I told him you were in Switzerland looking for some secret lost diary."

I pursed my lips, trying with all my might not to interrupt. My face became stern. I threw Miranda one of my disapproving looks.

"Why, what was I meant to say?" she said, raising her voice and becoming defensive.

"What did he say when you told him about the diary," I asked as a cold shiver ran down my spine.

"Well, unlike you now, he was really calm and interested. He thought it was amazing that you'd met his grandmother Tina and was blown away that I cracked the code of the matching lockets."

"What possessed you to tell him all of that?" I asked, trying hard not to be condescending.

"I don't know what your problem is," she snarled. "I thought you'd be happy for me. Happy I'd met a nice boy. Happy I'd met someone I have loads in common with. You're the one who said his grandmother was really lovely."

"I think she's right," Melody yelled out over the beaters as she whipped up her favourite cheesecake.

Miranda gave Melody one of her twin *thank you* smirks, pushed her chair back, slammed her mug down and stormed out.

The evening descended into deathly silence, not a word was uttered during dinner. I felt a surge of despair rising. I felt utterly lost and unsure of how to handle the situation.

That night as I lay awake, feeling out of my depth and unsettled, I tried to put myself in Miranda's shoes. I tried to remember the excitement of going on a first date. To be infatuated and giddy with excitement, waiting for the next encounter.

I great quote by Rumi came to mind: *"Yesterday I was clever, so I wanted to change the world. Today I am wise, so I am changing myself."*

I had been so busy lately, it felt like we were three galaxies spinning around under the same roof. I realised I hadn't actually told the girls they shouldn't discuss the diary with anyone.

So, over breakfast, I apologised and told Miranda I trusted her judgement and respected her decision to see Emilio. It was not for me to make judgements based simply on association.

She smiled, jumped up and gave me a big hug then they both left for school.

The rest of the day sailed by. Ruben sent a message saying work was manic and Isaac had gone skiing with his family and wouldn't be back until tomorrow.

I spent the morning in back-to-back meetings and the rest of the day working on files.

At 4:30 p.m., I was asked to attend a meeting with one of the senior partners to discuss a new project.

"Iris," Helen said, getting straight to the point, "now that the girls have almost finished school, we thought we'd discuss a new project and promotion. I'm aware in the past you've declined overseas travel opportunities, but we feel this is a perfect fit."

I didn't have a chance to comment, so I kept listening.

"As you know, our office in Milan is going through a period of rapid growth and expansion. We've just won a couple of major tenders and need someone with your skills and experience to head the department. Having a Dutch passport is a major advantage. You'd be in charge of a team of twenty others."

"I'm flattered," I said, "but the girls won't be going to uni until September."

"We're aware of that," Helen continued. "By the time we finish negotiations and engage our new clients, it will be May. We thought you could work remotely from London, flying to Milan one day per week until September and then reassess the situation."

I sat quietly, unsure how to respond.

"We'd appreciate you getting back to us within the next two weeks. If you decide to take the offer, you'd need to go to Milan for a day or two as an induction." With that, Helen abruptly left.

My head was in a spin. With everything going on with the diary, and Miranda with Emilio, I wasn't sure if it was wise to add Milan to my plate.

I thanked Helen, told her I was flattered and that I'd think about it.

CHAPTER 15

I told Ruben over a call this morning about Miranda and Emilio. As we discussed the coincidence of their meeting and Miranda disclosing the diary contents to Emilio Isaac interrupted our conversation and asked to speak to Ruben.

Isaac informed Ruben he'd placed an extensive spreadsheet with suppliers going back to 1945 into Dropbox. But because of privacy laws and the GDPR, he could not give him a list of old employees.

Ruben told me it would take quite a while to work his way through the list. He didn't think he'd have a chance until the weekend.

I told him not to worry and that I had a lot on my mind with the job offer. On top of that, I had to work out the new dilemma with the girls. I don't want to keep them in the dark about the diary, but at the same time, I don't

want Miranda to feed information straight to Emilio and
Hans Bokman Jr.

○ ○ ○

From: Ruben
To: Iris
Time: 7:00 p.m.

I've had a breakthrough. After running several filters
through the list, I discovered a man who supplied steel
from 1939 until 1982. His name was Jacob Lowe from
a company called "Lowe Mining & Steel." It fits perfectly
with what Leo Schmidt said.

*Mr Solomon held the key and supplied the infrastructure.
His genius successfully mined the minds of all the members.
He combined their strength and raw resources to create the
new material in the diary.*

It also matches what Mr Solomon's notes said.

*To steal the thoughts of others brings a new low to busi-
ness and humanity.*

xx

From: Iris
To: Ruben
Time: 7:05 p.m.

That's so amazing. You're a genius.

So how do we get hold of Jacob Lowe or his son?

Xx

From: Ruben

To: Iris

Time: 7:06 p.m.

That's where I've come to a roadblock. Lowe Mining & Steel seemed to have gone out of business in 1982.

All the subsequent searches I've done have no connection to Jacob Lowe.

Any suggestions?

Xx

From: Iris

To: Ruben

Time: 7:09 p.m.

Have you asked Isaac if he knew him?

Xx

From: Ruben

To: Iris

Time: 7:10 p.m.

Yes, he said that was before his time. He's never heard of him.

I then contacted Kurt in Belgium and asked if he'd remembered him at the meetings.

He said he heard people talk about Jacob Lowe. From memory, everyone spoke very highly of him. He can't remember if he had a wife or family.

Xx

From: Iris

To: Ruben

Time: 7:13 p.m.

OMG, you know what that means!! The only person left who would know is...... Tina Bokman, the mother of Hans Bokman Jr., grandmother of Emilio Bokman, who has just started dating my daughter.

AWKWARD!!

Xx

CHAPTER 16

The last couple of days, I've lived in a constant state of turmoil. The more I thought about my dilemma with work and telling the girls about the diary, the more my anxiety increased. Finally, last night I decided to lay my cards on the table and had an open, honest conversation with the girls. We discussed my work and the Milan opportunity. We made a list of positive and negatives, including the impact on all of our lives. I remembered to constantly ask them what their thoughts were and if they had any solutions. I was very impressed with their maturity. I think they felt reassured I included them in the decision-making processes. I believe that we surpassed our communication evolution last night. We resolved to sleep on all our suggestions and discuss all points again next week.

I thought it best to leave the diary until another time when everyone was feeling respected and understood.

I'm glad I did. I was also still in two minds, whether I was going to pursue the last section.

At breakfast, they asked about Davos and Leo Schmidt. I thought there was no harm in telling them about the section on observing time and space.

"So why don't you want to look for the next section?" Melody asked curious by my sudden lack of enthusiasm.

I explained we had no leads and didn't know what to do next. The last person who knew Jacob Lowe seems to have died, and we can't figure out who may have the information. We're not sure if Jacob had a wife or children. It appears we've come to a dead end.

Sharp as a tack, Miranda piped up, "Why don't you ask Tina Bokman? She said she'd love to hear from you. She also seems to know everyone associated with David Solomon and is probably the last one left from the secret meetings who's still alive."

I smiled and said, "Yes, I'd thought of that, too, but I wasn't sure how to go about asking her."

"Seems pretty simple to me. Why don't you call her like you did before and ask her. How hard can it be, Mum?" Miranda asked, smirking.

"She does have a point," Melody said, giving Miranda a wink.

I agreed and said I'd call her later.

I decided not to mention Emilio directly. Instead, I came at it from another angle.

With a serious, authoritative tone, I said to the girls, "I think we owe it to the people who wrote the diary not to discuss the contents with anyone other than ourselves. As you know, they went to an enormous amount of effort to keep the diary secret. A lot of people lost their lives during the war due to psychological warfare. Until we have the full contents of the diary and understand how and why it can harm others, please promise me you'll keep the information to yourself."

They both said they understood and wouldn't mention it to anyone.

With that, Melody went off to start her new dog walking business with the dog next door, and Miranda went to meet Emilio to go rock climbing.

Having finished my coffee and cleared my head, I decided to call Tina Bokman.

I was relieved that, after several rings, she finally picked up. She was an absolute delight and put all my fears to rest. She thought it was a hoot that Miranda and Emilio had gone to the movies together and was simply delighted to hear they were rock climbing today. She said she was so proud of Emilio—such a bright boy with a lot of potential, she said. Just like his grandfather.

I finally plucked up the courage to ask if she'd heard of Jacob Lowe. The line went silent. After a long pause, I said, "Hello, are you still there, Mrs Bokman?"

"Yes, I am, my dear. I see you've made progress with the diary."

"Yes, I have, but I've come to a dead end. I know you promised not to divulge any further information, but I wondered if you could be so kind as to let me know about Jacob Lowe. You're not technically telling me anything about the diary. You're just telling me about people my grandparents knew and perhaps helped during the war."

"That's an interesting way of looking at it, dearie," she said. "I think it would be fine to fill you in on life in the camp and the friendships we made." Tina paused and continued," Jacob Lowe was a very down to earth man, uncomplicated, with the most impeccable morals and ethics. Before the war, he owned a successful mining company and was the primary steel and iron ore supplier to Solomon Steel. He and his wife Margriet arrived in the camp shortly after Mr Solomon. Margriet and David Solomon's sister Ada were best friends as children. Unfortunately, Margriet was unable to have children."

"What work did Jacob and Margriet do in the camp?" I asked.

"Jacob did manual labour work, and Margriet was a nurse. She spent a lot of time with the orphaned children. When they left the camp, they adopted a young girl named Frieda Amiel, who was seven at the time. I remember little Frieda would play with your mother for hours in your grandparents' front garden. I often saw them playing ball and skip rope."

"Did you stay in contact with them after the war?"

"Of course, we became the best of friends over the three years we were in the camp together. Sadly, Jacob and Margriet passed away within months of each other in 1982."

"What about Frieda? Have you stayed in contact with her?" I asked, secretly hoping she had.

"Yes, we speak a couple of times a year and always send each other birthday and Christmas cards," she shared warmly.

"I'd really appreciate it if you could give me Frieda's details so I can contact her about the last section," I said, hardly able to contain my excitement.

After a long pause, Tina replied, "No, I'm sorry, I can't do that. However, I can contact Frieda myself and explain why you'd like to speak to her. She's a very busy influential woman. I respect her privacy and her time." Tina then firmly requested, "Please give me your details and I will pass them on to Frieda. She will contact you in due course if she feels that is the correct way forward."

I was a little surprised and taken aback by her response but had to respect her wishes.

The rest of the conversation covered some idle chit chat. I thanked Mrs Bokman once again for her time and kindness in helping me with my search.

○ ○ ○

It was around 10:30 a.m the following Tuesday when I came across an interesting email from Margaret Brown. I had found the last couple of days to be extraordinarily uneventful. I kept looking at my phone for missed calls and searching my inbox. Not hearing from Frieda Amiel made me realise I did want to find the final section of the diary. I'd never checked my spam folder as regularly as the past couple of days. It was during one of these email searches that I spotted Margaret's most recent email to me.

From: Margaret Brown
To: Iris
    Hi Iris,
    I've got more gossip on Hans Bokman Jr.
    While I was at a City of London Business Meeting last night, I overheard Hans Bokman gloating that he'd just come back from a sailing trip with an influential MP. The trip was a huge success. Yesterday he signed a £30 million contract to install his industrial air pollution and waste-water filters on government sites to reduce the pollution levels in Central London. Not only that, he said he'd raised £20 million in crowdfunding to build a factory to manufacture the filters, which he guarantees are 100% effective in removing chemical waste and toxins from air and water.
    Can you believe it?
    Best Margaret

From: Iris
To: Margaret Brown
    Hi Margaret,
    Thanks for the update. Got to hand it to Hans; he's got the charm and prowess of a snake oil salesman.
    Got time for a sneaky lunch?
    Best
    Iris

My phone pinged and I read and answered a message from Ruben:

From: Ruben
To: Iris

Hi Rissy,

How's it going? Have you heard anything from Frieda?

Do you have a backup plan in case she doesn't get in touch?

Isaac just asked me to fly out to Western Australia to speak to some potential new suppliers. I'm leaving on Thursday. I'll be gone for ten days. I arrive Saturday morning, so I will have time to see Sarah and the kids in Sydney first.

Have you decided what to do about the Milan offer?

R xx

From: Iris
To: Ruben

Hi Rubes,

No haven't heard anything yet. No backup plan either.

I still haven't decided on Milan.

I did hear some interesting gossip on Hans Bokman Jr.; remind me to tell you when we chat.

How exciting about WA. So lovely you can see Sarah and the kids.

Rissy xx

I smiled and looked up from my phone at my laptop screen, only to see a new email notification pop up at the right-hand corner. I looked closely and did a double take. The sender was Frieda Acciaio.

10:37 p.m.
From: Frieda Acciaio
To: Iris De Angelo
Dear Iris,

I was delighted to hear from Tina Bokman the other day. She told me about your quest to find the secret diary.

However, her call took me by surprise, and I'm in two minds about how to proceed.

I would be pleased to meet you in person and enjoy hearing more about your mother and what happened after the war.

You are more than welcome to visit me just outside of Milan, where I reside.

I look forward to hearing from you.
Yours faithfully
Frieda Acciaio.

Frieda's email turned my world upside down. My head was going off like fireworks; one thought instantly brought on another, and then another. I kept wondering what she would be like in person? Would she be prickly? Would she cross-examine me on what I know about the diary? Would she quiz me about what my intentions are for the diary?

My old friends, Fear and Doubt, had crept back in and were on fire. Do I actually want to meet her? Is it worth going to Milan to be drilled by Frieda?

I decided it was best to wait to reply. I had absolutely no idea what to say. I needed some time to gather my rampant thoughts.

I finally fell asleep sometime after 3 a.m. but my restless, sleep-deprived night did nothing for my mood or ability to make rational decisions. I decided now was not the time to make life-changing decisions. Instead, when I finally rose from my bed, I sent Frieda a cautious message.

9:37 a.m.
From: Iris De Angelo
To: Frieda Acciaio

Dear Frieda,

Thank you very much for contacting me. I understand and appreciate your concerns about divulging details of the secret diary.

I think it's important you understand, I'm not simply interested in learning the diary's contents. My world has been completely transformed since visiting Camp Westerbork.

I have learnt more about my grandparents' history during the war in the past couple of weeks than in my entire lifetime.

I'm ashamed to say I hardly knew anything about their time in the transit camp or about the people they helped save from going on the extermination trains.

It would be an honour and delight to meet with you and hear your story. Tina mentioned you were a young girl whilst in the camp and you knew my mother. I would love to hear more about your memories and how your life was shaped during your time in the camp.

Please let me know when is convenient for us to meet in person?

Yours faithfully

Iris De Angelo

Little did I realise that one email would catapult my life in a whole new direction. Helen was over the moon when I'd agree to go to Milan to speak to the team. Ruben was pleased I hadn't given up on the diary, and the girls were ecstatic. I finally let go and trust them to stay home alone for a couple of days.

CHAPTER 17

The flight from London to Milan only took two hours, and to my joy we were not held in a holding pattern circling Milan waiting for a slot to land. I was hoping this was a sign of things to come.

The weather certainly didn't disappoint—a gorgeous sunny day, and not a cloud in the sky. I felt exhilarated peeling off my heavy coat and slipping on my sunglasses and hat. A bit of sunshine truly is the elixir for the winter blues. I could definitely get used to this way of life, I thought.

A driver met me at the airport and took me straight to the business district in Milan's city centre. Our office is located in the up-and-coming location of Porta Nuova, in a recently completed high rise building. The view is most definitely worth writing home about.

I met my potential new team who were very enthusiastic and seemed genuinely passionate about their work.

One of the partners introduced me to the rest of the staff then showed me around town. I could instantly see why it's one of Europe's richest city centres.

Over a simple but sumptuous bowl of pasta in a small restaurant close to the office, we discussed logistics and strategy. I sadly had to decline to see the Duomo Cathedral and Leonardo da Vinci's *Last Supper* in Santa Maria Delle Grazi, as I'd promised Frieda I'd meet her in Lake Como at 4 p.m. If only I'd given myself more time in Milan, I thought.

The train to Lake Como took just under an hour. I kept pinching myself to make sure it was real. Was it really possible to work part-time in Milan? Could I start a new chapter in my career, allowing me to enjoy the cuisine, the museums and galleries in Milan? Would it be OK to leave the girls in the UK whilst I worked in Milan? Do they honestly need me there every day now that they're about to start uni?

Before I knew it, Frieda's driver met me at the station and drove me to her villa, which was right on Lake Como, opposite the Bellagio peninsula at the foothills of the Alps. Driving through her stately gates with an imposing family crest in black and gold, I couldn't but notice the breathtaking views of the lake. We continued down a steep pebble stone driveway past an elegantly designed ornamental garden and pulled up in front of her majestic three storey 17th century liberty-style villa.

Frieda led me through the foyer past Baroque paintings, luxuriously upholstered furnishings and the most beautiful Venetian chandelier to her terrace garden.

She instantly put my fears to rest. Over a delightful light supper, we caught up on her time in Westerbork and what life had in store for her after the war.

Frieda explained she entered the camp with her parents when she was only four years old. She remembers there being chaos when they arrived in the camp. Nobody knew what was going on. They waited and slept in a large room with hundreds of other prisoners for two days and two nights until they were registered and issued with ID passes. Once registered and stripped of all their belongings, they were allocated a dormitory that housed several other families.

"If you don't mind me asking, where did you live before the war?" I asked. "And what were your parents' occupations?"

"We lived in The Hague," Frieda explained. "My father, Abraham Amiel, was a famous artist. His paintings depicted interior family scenes showing every day domestic life. My mother looked after me and helped my father with the administration of his business. I believe he painted your grandparents and your mother in the living room in their home in Westerbork."

I looked at her in outright shock. A shiver ran down my spine.

"I can't believe what you're telling me. I have that painting. It was given to me when my grandfather passed away a couple of years ago. It's hanging proudly on my living room wall just in front of my grandmother's chair, the one that's actually in the painting."

Frieda looked down then gave me a reassuring smile.

"What work did your parents do during their time at Westerbork?" I asked.

"My father was a painter; he was responsible for painting the new buildings as they expanded the camp to house more prisoners. My mother was a seamstress and continually repaired uniforms and inmates' clothes," Frieda explained.

"I'm sorry to ask, but what led to you become an orphan?" I asked, trying to be as sensitive as possible.

"Two years and three months after entering the camp, when I was six and a half years old, I fell ill with measles and was placed in isolation in the hospital. My parents could only see me from a distance. One morning when my parents didn't come to visit before work, I was astonished to discover my parents' names had been placed on the list to go on the trains leaving the camp. At the time, nobody knew where these trains were going. I was told my parents had gone to another camp for work and would come back to get me."

"Do you know why their names went on the list?" I asked, confused.

"After many years of sending prisoners to the extermination camps, the numbers in the camp had substantially reduced. People like your grandfather could no longer keep my parents on the essential worker list as there was no need for their labour. There was a lot of commotion when they got on the train as my name wasn't on the list. Someone overheard my parents say, 'Leave it, she's safer here.' They said they would come back for me later."

"What happened when you were well enough to leave the hospital?"

"I was placed in an orphanage within the camp with several other children," Frieda answered.

"How long did you spend in the orphanage?" I asked.

"Nine very long months. There were twenty-five of us at the time ranging from a baby boy only a couple of months old to a beautiful young girl who was twelve years old."

"What did you do while you were in the orphanage?"

"I went to a small school where one of the teachers was your grandmother. Your 'Oma' was the kindest, most caring teacher I'd ever come across. After school, she invited me to her home and let me play with your mother. It made my grief and yearning for my parents more tolerable."

"That's amazing you still got an education," I said, pleased to be learning so much more about the camp.

"Yes, the camp administrators, which included your grandfather, ensured all the children continued to get an education, got exercise and had religious classes," Frieda replied with a gentle nod. "We had many professors, famous musicians, and rabbis within the camp to educate us. One of our most dedicated teachers was Mr Elijah Finkelstein; he loved all his students unconditionally. When a number of children were placed on the list to go on the train, Mr Finkelstein said he would go with them even though his name wasn't on the list. He wanted to make sure they arrived safely. We found out some time after liberation that Mr Finkelstein had gone to Auschwitz and gassed along with the children."

"How terribly sad," I said, feeling heartbroken to hear her tragic childhood unfold, and then asked, "What happened at the end of the war when Holland was liberated?"

"Many of the orphaned children were adopted by the prisoners within the camp. Mr and Mrs Lowe kindly adopted me."

"How was it decided that they would adopt you?" I asked.

"After my parents went on the trains, Margriet Lowe, the nurse who looked after me in the hospital, came to see me daily in the orphanage. I spent many hours listening to her stories about her life before entering the camp. As time went on, we became very close, and eventually, I saw her as a mother figure. It was only natural by the time we left the camp they would look after me and help me find my parents," Frieda explained.

"Did it take long to find out what happened?" I asked.

"For me, it seemed to take an eternity. Jacob and Margriet put their heart and soul into trying to locate them. It was a harrowing, drawn-out, emotional roller-coaster ride. Many people tried to help. Everyone seemed to want to give positive news. Someone said they spent time with them in Auschwitz, and they were transferred to another camp; someone else said they managed to escape. Eventually, the truth came out; they were sent to the gas chambers three months after arrival."

"I'm truly sorry to hear about your heartbreaking childhood and time in Westerbork," I said, really unsure what else to say.

"It's OK, Iris," Frieda assured. "I'm not the only one who suffered. It was a very long time ago. I remember my father Abraham saying every night before he kissed me good-night, *'What is to give light must endure burning.'* Many wonderful things came out of the tragedy. I couldn't have asked for more loving surrogate parents. We filled a void in each other's lives."

"I'm intrigued; Lake Como is a long way from Rotterdam. What brought you here?" I asked.

"I believe you're aware Jacob Lowe had mines before the war and supplied David Solomon with iron ore and steel." When I nodded, Frieda continued, "As the Lowe's never had children, I naturally worked in the business from a young age and eventually took over the business. When I was twenty-five, I attended an industry confer-ence in Rotterdam, and I met a handsome young Italian man called Lorenzo Acciaio. We felt an instant connection and a deep attraction. His family also owned mines; theirs were in Italy and throughout Africa. The difficulty was he lived in Milan, and I lived in Rotterdam. For 18 months, we maintained a long-distance relationship. We eventu-ally married in Lake Como at the Villa d'Este in 1965."

"Where did you live after you got married?" I asked Frieda.

"Lorenzo and I moved to Milan as he was the oldest son and was learning to take over the family business from his father," she explained. "I stopped working for approxi-mately ten years while I raised our sons Fabrizio and Guido. In 1982 sadly, my father, Jacob Lowe, passed away from cancer, and a couple of months later, my mother died of a broken heart."

"What happened to Lowe Mines and Steel?"

"We weren't sure what to do about Lowe Mines and Steel as our life was in Milan, and we didn't want to relocate to Holland. We also had the business to run here. After a lot of heated discussions and lengthy negotiations with Lorenzo's family, we decided to merge the two businesses, and the rest they say is history."

I smiled to myself; that makes a lot of sense—no wonder Ruben couldn't find Lowe Mines and Steel on his spreadsheet.

We continued catching up on the past until late in the evening. I was in utter awe of Frieda and her story, so much so I completely forgot to ask her about the diary.

Just as Frieda was taking me to the guest bedroom, she said, "Tomorrow we can go to Bellagio, and I'll explain about the diary."

I couldn't stop smiling.

CHAPTER 18

I woke to the delightful smell of fresh coffee permeating through my door. Feeling surprisingly at peace and well-rested, I went over our conversation from last night in my head. I had questions, but they didn't seem urgent. Frieda's honesty and openness last night reassured me that everything was unfolding exactly as it should be.

After a nourishing breakfast of fresh fruit and yoghurt, we climbed on board her luxury Como classic wooden boat and motored along the lake towards Bellagio. The weather was slightly cooler than yesterday but still warm and sunny with bright blue skies.

As we cruised along the lake looking at the enormous villas of past and present famous people, Frieda explained Jacob Lowe and David Solomon had been very close, in fact like brothers. David's sister Ada and Margriet had been best friends since they met in school at age five.

When Margriet met Jacob, she introduced him to Ada and David Solomon. It didn't take long before they would all socialise together.

"In Westerbork, the Lowes and Solomons were very supportive of each other," Frieda told me. "At the time David was asked to chair the secret meetings about the diary, he knew without a shadow of a doubt that Jacob would provide invaluable insights. My father, Jacob, shared stories with me about what happened in the meetings, the reason for the secrecy was the fear of releasing the contents to a world that wasn't ready."

Frieda confirmed her father Jacob was the guardian of the last section of the diary, which discussed 'Understanding'.

She then went on to explain in depth the section on 'Understanding':

5. Understanding—The fifth principle in Communication Intelligence

My destination is no longer a location, but a new way of conscious understanding.

Our future is determined, in large part, by the choices we make now.

We cannot always control our circumstances, but we can and do choose our response to whatever arises.

"The final section described a new understanding of conscious behaviour," she elaborated. "Just before the war, there had been a surge of study and discovery within the fields of psychology, neuroscience, sociology, and behavioural science. For the most part, the knowledge and findings remained an intellectual concept discussed and debated purely within intellectual circles of influence. They understood the key to ending human conflict but also realised this knowledge was a double-edged sword. The same knowledge could and did create unprecedented global tragedy, psychological warfare, and the Holocaust. The diary states once you become conscious of yourself and others, it will set you free."

I nodded affirmatively. Making sure I took in every word.

"Can you explain what you mean by conscious of yourself and others?" I said, not entirely understanding what she meant.

"As you learnt in the first section, humans are constantly evolving along with technology. Up until now, human evolution has been mostly unconscious. Major events such as wars and now the pandemic have forced the human race to re-evaluate its unconscious behaviour."

"Yes, but how do we make our unconscious behaviour conscious?" I asked.

"Understanding this section is truly powerful and will set you free. Conscious understanding in an important ingredient of peace of mind. Without peace of mind nothing else will matter. You can measure how well you're doing at any point in time by the amount of peace of mind you enjoy. Becoming conscious and aware of your communication and interaction with others and the environment is very much like being on this lake. You can either drift along like that branch over there, unconscious, with no direction, or you can consciously get in a boat and steer it in the direction you want to go. Understanding that you have a choice is fundamental to your success."

"That makes a lot of sense," I said, "but there is so much to understand. I can never fully understand, let alone remember all the psychological terms to use to be conscious of my communication and interactions with people."

"Yes, I understand," Frieda said sympathetically. "You don't have to remember all the science behind your actions and communication. Just like you don't need to need to know the physics behind why this boat floats or the technology and mechanics behind the engine and steering mechanism. It's more important to be aware of fundamental rules to follow to be safe and keep others safe."

"Can you explain what conscious communication means?" I asked, battling to come to terms with what she was saying.

"Understanding conscious communication is as simple as understanding common courtesies. Respecting others, listening, being polite and patient, and not interrupting are all basics manners every nation and religion support and encourage. Being mindful of these basic concepts will go a long way to reducing human conflict and help integrate the world from east to west. It's unfortunate in our fast-paced world, of striving for success, these basic principles have been forgotten."

"I'm still confused. I understand about common courtesies, but I'm not sure where I should start," I said, leaning back in my chair, looking at the drifting branch.

"It's important to start with ourselves. To become aware of our life story and the unconscious act, we play out daily. Are you constantly short of time, talking quickly, multi-tasking, looking at a phone or device whilst attempting to listen to others? Are you abrupt and tend to cut people off? Or are you more aloof, withdrawn, and non-engaging? Do you tend to talk a lot and never allow others to speak? Are you headstrong and determined? Are you constantly late?"

"Does that mean being aware of your reputation and your web shadow?" I asked.

"Yes, once you become conscious of who you are and your habits, your life will take off. Conflicts will dissipate like the ripples on this lake."

"How will I know if I'm on the right path to conscious communication?" I asked, trying to put all her information into perspective.

"Think back to a time when a conversation seemed to flow, and you felt connected," Frieda suggested.

I told her about my conversation with Ruben in St Moritz at Mathis restaurant.

"How did you feel?" she asked.

I had to stop and think. "Alive, happy, I suppose."

"What else?" Frieda asked encouragingly.

"I think, yes, I definitely felt connected, I felt light and respected. We were wholeheartedly interested in what the other said. We gave each other time and space to answer. There was no rush or competition to outdo the story of the other. It felt like our conversation had meaning and purpose."

Frieda continued, "That is the key, right there. You should remember that conversation as your point of reference. Remember all the things that were important to you, such as feeling connected and respected, then reciprocate that behaviour when you communicate with others."

"OK, but how will I remember to do that, especially when I'm busy or rushed?" I asked, trying not to sound too negative.

"As I said earlier, you need to become aware of the times you aren't conscious of your behaviour, such as when you are in a hurry," Frieda reiterated. "Before humans can reach the next level of communication expansion, we need to end the period of self-absorption and short-sighted behaviour. We need to develop our empathy to expedite not only our own but everyone's evolution."

Just as I was mulling over what Frieda had said, we arrived at Bellagio. The captain pulled up in front of a gorgeous terraced café that seemed full of regulars who had already claimed the best tables on the waterfront. As we approached, Frieda waved to a handsome, elegantly dressed man about my age. He stood up when we arrived and held out his hand.

"Hello Iris, my name is Fabrizio; I'm delighted to meet you," he said, smiling broadly. "I hope you don't mind if I join you for lunch with my mother."

I suddenly felt very self-conscious and underdressed in my casual floral dress, with a wide belt and full skirt.

"Lovely to meet you, Fabrizio," I said. This is a pleasant surprise, I thought.

Fabrizio pulled out my chair and waited to push it in. I noticed he was not only charming but used old school etiquette.

He'd been waiting at a table with the most sensational view of the lake in the perfect balance of sun and shade. It was apparent this wasn't his first time here. The waiter addressed him by his first name and gave him his 'usual lunch'. I felt like I was in a Hollywood movie, sitting on the edge of my seat waiting for the director to say at any moment—'cut'.

Fabrizio instantly put me at ease. He was extremely attentive in a genuinely interested kind of way. It was self-evident he'd been taught the principles of conscious understanding mentioned in the diary. He was 100% focused and attentive not only to our conversation but the environment. Fabrizio noticed when my glass was empty and immediately filled it up; he passed the salt as I reached for it. With no effort at all, he read all my body language and cues. Fabrizio handed me a napkin when I needed to wipe my hands. He asked if I wanted to swap chairs and sit in the shade when he saw me getting hot. He wasn't in any hurry to rush off somewhere else. I was fascinated by the power of reciprocity. His immaculate manners and gentle calm nature led to a feeling of trust and honesty. I realised I'd unconsciously matched his mannerisms and emotional state.

After lunch, Frieda excused herself telling us she still had a few errands to run. Fabrizio said he would drop me back to his parents' villa.

Fabrizio was completely open and forthright and not afraid to show his emotions. He explained how his wife Sofia, had sadly passed away thirteen months ago from stomach cancer. She was the most energetic, vibrant woman, he told me as he reminisced. A lover of life, she was a fantastic cook and loved to dance. She would light up a room the moment she entered. They'd been married for over twenty-three years.

"I fully understand what you're going through," I said. "If you don't mind me asking, how have you managed on your own?"

"It's been quite an adjustment not having her around," Fabrizio confessed. "I'm incredibly grateful for the help of my entire family, especially my mother. In September, I went through another significant change in my life when my younger son left home to join his older brother in Rome. They're both at university; Giovanni, my older son, is studying Business, and my younger son Luca is studying Robotics."

Without realising the time, we chatted until sunset. Fabrizio took me back to his parents' villa and then drove me back to Milan airport.

Before I left for Milan, Frieda handed me an envelope. She said she was most impressed and extremely pleased it was me that had found all the sections of the diary. It was a double sign from the universe that my destiny was attached to the diary. She told me Iris was the Greek Goddess of Communication and De Angelo means Angel or Messenger.

Frieda wished me the very best and said the envelope's details would lead me to the actual diary if that was my destiny.

○ ○ ○

I finally arrived home at 10 p.m. to find the girls very excited to see me. Well, so I initially thought.

"Hi girls, I'm back," I said as I entered the door.

"Hi Mum," Miranda said, skipping down the stairs.

"Where's Melody?" I asked.

"Oh, she's giving Henry the vacuum cleaner a head transplant."

"Sorry," I said. "What happened now?" Deep breath, remain calm, ask questions, I thought to myself.

"Well. It seems like another one of Melody's experiments went wrong," Miranda said, hardly containing her fits of laughter.

"What experiment was that?" I asked whilst putting my luggage down and the kettle on.

"I'll be there in a sec, Mum," Melody yelled out from the living room. "It's my story—let me tell it!" she yelled out to Miranda.

Once Melody arrived, she began to explain herself. "So Mum, it's like this," she said confidently. "Yesterday, I was in the living room and saw a mouse run under Oma's chair. I didn't want to hurt it, so I decided to use the vacuum cleaner in a reverse cycle to blow air out instead of sucking air in. I thought the air would push the mouse out from under the chair, and then I could blow it out the door. Like you see gardeners blow leaves."

"Unfortunately, it didn't work," Miranda butted in, giggling profusely.

"So, what happened?" I asked. Afraid of what I may hear.

"Well, when I blasted the air under the chair, the mouse ran out and up my leg. I threw the vacuum cleaner down, screaming and ran off trying to get rid of the mouse. The chair fell over onto the vacuum cleaner and smashed the head."

"Oh my god, you should have seen it, Mum, it was so funny. I couldn't stop laughing," Miranda said. "If only I'd videoed it. It would have gone viral on YouTube."

"What happened to the vacuum cleaner?" I said, not sure I wanted to know at 10:30 p.m.

Melody said proudly, "Well, the good news is the chair is absolutely fine. But, poor Henry, the vacuum cleaner wasn't so good," she added, showing genuine remorse. "But, don't worry, Mum, the delivery man came earlier, and I've fixed him. I successfully gave him a head transplant; we expect him to make a full recovery and be back cleaning in 24-48 hours." She grinned with the sheer delight of a budding surgeon.

After giving me a brief demonstration and catching up on their highlights of the last few days, I fell into bed exhausted, pleased our little home had survived another twin-ado. I decided to wait until tomorrow to open Frieda's envelope.

CHAPTER 19

How nice it was to sleep in, knowing I had found the last section of the diary. It gave me a sense of calm and relief. I was riding a high from Lake Como, with everything coming together. Frieda had made me feel like one of the family. She willingly shared all she knew about her time in Camp Westerbork, about the diary and what she thought about the contents. Her words kept resounding in my head:

'Knowledge becomes like the slimy water at the bottom of a vase if it's not given the opportunity to flow.'

I couldn't but wonder, am I meant to find the actual diary?

Am I meant to share the contents of the diary with the world? Is my name a sign that my life path is entwined with the Fourth Dimension in Communication?

Memories of my grandparents came flooding back. Tears began to well as I remember our happy times together. Our family gatherings were always very loud, bubbling over with excitement and laughter. My grandparents, parents, aunts, uncles, and cousins found any excuse to celebrate with a lot of food. My mother had a calendar on the back to the toilet door, which logged everyone's birthday. We seemed to be together at least one Sunday a month. History was told and history was made at these wonderful celebrations. I remember my grandmother excelled at storytelling and wove a moral or quote into her enchanting narratives. One such quote kept coming back to me, over and over again.

'One moment can change a day,
One day can change a life,
One life can change the world.'

My glorious trip down memory lane was abruptly cut short with the girls shouting out that breakfast was ready. They'd made a sumptuous feast of Eggs Benedict with only a tiny portion of the fry pan handle melting. Breakfast was a sheer delight, besides the lingering smell of burnt plastic.

During breakfast, I told them about Milan and the lovely people in the office. I told them I was seriously thinking of accepting the position. I explained about Frieda and her time in Camp Westerbork and that her father had painted the picture we have in the living room of Great Oma and Great Opa.

"What did she say about the diary?" Miranda asked, filling her glass with orange juice.

"She said the last section of the diary outlined conscious understanding. It means we have a choice how we communicate with others, and these choices have consequences."

"What else did she say about the sections?" the girls asked in unison.

"She said the last section in the diary pulls all the sections together and gives a powerful model of communication that is exceptionally easy to implement."

"So, where's the diary" Miranda asked whilst looking at her phone and sending another message.

"That's just it; I still don't know. Frieda gave me this envelope just before I left her villa and said this would lead to the diary."

"So, what does it say?" Melody asked, leaning forward to see inside the envelope.

"It says:

'Life is always at a turning point.

   What lies behind us and what lies before us are small matters compared to what lies within us.

   Your destiny will be revealed when you follow the sign of the bull.' "

"Oh great," Miranda said with a sigh. "Another riddle. I don't have time for this. I need to go to the High Street and return some clothes, and then I've arranged to meet Emilio for a hot chocolate at 4 p.m. at Tilly's Tea House."

"That's fine," I said. "I need to speak to Ruben and update him on all that's happened. What's your plan for today, Melody?" I asked whilst clearing the table.

She replied, "I'm free to help solve the riddle. I was going to finish my art project, but it doesn't need to be in for another week."

I was unable to get hold of Ruben because he was in transit somewhere in Australia. I had left a message and so decided to brainstorm with Melody. Meanwhile, Miranda was wandering in and out of the living room, sending messages.

"Let's try and figure out what could be at a turning point?"

"Driving a car, a movie, and an old record player?" Melody said enthusiastically.

"OK that's a start. Let's move on to the next sentence."

"What lies before us, behind us and within us?" I said.

"Air," Miranda shouted out. "Ha ha ha."

"That could work," I said.

"Any suggestions for the sign of the bull?"

"Oh my god, yes!" Miranda said, full of enthusiasm. "It could be a Taurus astrology sign. That's a bull. What have we got that has a Taurus symbol on it?"

"Excellent idea," I said.

"Doesn't it say the 'sign' of the bull?" Melody corrected.

"In our history of art class, Miss Turner said that many famous paintings had people using their hands to give a sign, one of them was the sign of the bull," Melody said excitedly.

"What does the sign of the bull look like?" I asked, puzzled.

"It's where the pinkie and index finger are up, and all the other fingers are down. It looks like a horn," Melody said, proud of her contribution.

All of a sudden, Miranda jumped up and cried, "I've got it! It's so obvious and staring us in the face."

"What is?" I said, getting more confused by the minute.

"The riddle, it's right before our eyes," Miranda said, rolling her eyes. "Frieda could only write that note because she knew with confidence that you would be able to find it. Right?"

"I suppose," I said, still unsure where this was leading.

"Well, think about it. What connects Frieda with us?" she said, getting louder and more excited.

"Look at the picture her father painted. Great-grandma is sitting in the chair with grandma on her lap. Great-grandpa is standing behind the chair at an angle, turning towards the chair. Look at his fingers; they're in the sign of the bull. He's pointing at great-grandma who's in this very chair."

Melody ran towards the chair. "I bet it's in here. When I knocked the chair over yesterday trying to save the mouse, I noticed it had been repaired under the seat. The stitching there was different from the rest of the stitching."

We all ran towards the chair, turned it over and sure enough, there was unusual stitching. It felt like there could be something inside. Miranda ran off to get the biggest pair of scissors she could find.

I slowly undid the stitches. The excitement was unbearable. My stomach was in knots.

I was shaking, unsure if I wanted to find the diary after all.

When all the stitches were undone, we looked inside with great anticipation.

We were dumbfounded. There wasn't anything in there except stuffing and springs.

"That doesn't make sense," I said. I felt sure we'd cracked the code.

"Hang on a minute. Let's reread the riddle," Melody said, staring back at the picture.

'Life is always at a turning point.

What lies behind us and what lies before us are small matters compared to what lies within us.

Your destiny will be revealed when you follow the sign of the bull.'

"Let me try turning the chair and go deeper into it," Melody suggested. She knelt to get a better look. "I can see something in the back section," she said, her voice rising with trepidation. "There's something in the middle of the spine section."

Melody rattled around for a while before calling out, "Miranda, quick, get my phone, so I can take a picture with the flash." Her sister ran to get it for her and Melody took a quick, bright photo. She examined it and said, "There's definitely something in there," sounding euphoric. "Mum, quick, can you get the tongs from the kitchen?" she asked, getting ready to go deep within the chair.

Miranda and I gathered around the chair, trying hard not to rip it apart, as Melody undertook her second operation for the week. Ever so slowly and gently, she wiggled the tongs up into the chair. It wasn't an easy operation. The tongs kept slipping, and she'd come up empty-handed. After what seemed like an eternity, she finally managed to get a good grip and give birth to a brown envelope with something heavy inside.

We waited with bated breath to see the contents.

I couldn't believe my eyes. My body was covered in goosebumps. Sitting right in front of us was the diary written in 1945. It was made of beautiful soft brown leather with leather stitching on the side.

"Mum, look, there's a lock on the side," Miranda exclaimed. "How are you going to open it? Do you have the key?"

"Oh, great. No, how am I supposed to have the key?" I said, feeling deflated.

"Hang on didn't you say you'd found a few keys in that tin box at David Solomon's work?" Melody piped up.

"Yes, we did, actually, but I think Ruben kept them after opening the box at Roland Boerman's farm near Westerbork," I said, trying to remember.

"Um, no, he didn't," Miranda said blushing.

"What do you mean?" I asked, baffled.

"I may have borrowed your new handbag while you were in Milan and found some secret pocket with old keys in it," Miranda said sheepishly.

"Where are the keys now?" I asked, not sure whether to be angry or ecstatic.

"Where you left them," she said with conviction.

"Could you get them for me, please?"

Miranda triumphantly handed over the bunch of old keys from my handbag.

"Can I try?" Miranda said with hope in her eyes.

"Why not, but gently," I said.

We went through five keys, each time becoming more disappointed until finally, we had a match. Ever so slowly and gently, the key turned, and the lock sprung open.

Inside the diary, we discovered a lot of careful swirly old writing in blue ink. It was very neatly written in defined sections.

"How come it's written in English?" Miranda said, breaking our silence.

"That's an excellent question, Miranda. I'm not sure," I said.

"Well, if they wanted it to be a secret and they were in a Dutch prisoner of war camp, then it makes sense to write it in another language," Melody said, leaning her head forward to get a better look. "At least it's not written in some other code."

Just then, my phone rang. It was Ruben in Australia.

I excused myself and left the girls to investigate the diary while I spent the next forty-five minutes catching up about Australia and my travels to Milan and Lake Como. Ruben told me about Sarah and the kids and how lovely it was to spend quality time together. He was fascinated to hear about the last section of the diary and amazed that we'd found it in my grandmother's chair. We arranged to chat again tomorrow once I'd had a chance to go through the contents of the diary.

By the time I got off the phone and returned to the living room, Miranda was gone. Melody seemed to be in a state of panic.

"What's wrong?" I asked. "You have a look of dread on your face. And where's Miranda?"

"She's gone to meet Emilio on the High Street—and it looks like she's taken the diary!"

"What! How?" I cried. "Tell me what you know."

"Miranda told me she was going to meet Emilio and while she was getting ready to leave, I saw a message flash up on her phone. It said, 'So amazing can't wait to see it. Make sure you bring it.'—something like that. The next thing I knew, she'd left, and now I can't find the diary."

"You have *got* to be kidding?" I said, absolutely livid. "After everything everyone has done to keep it secret. The elders were so fearful of the details getting into the wrong hands, especially Hans Bokman and now Miranda's handing it straight to his son. This is a disaster. What are we going to do?"

"Leave it with me, Mum. I've got an idea, but I have to leave now!" Melody yelled back as she flew out the door with a package under her arm.

Two hours later, they both returned. Having mastered the art of neutral body language. I had to wait patiently to find out what happened.

Stay calm and keep asking questions, I kept telling myself.

"OK, can someone please explain what's going on?" I said, trying hard to remain calm. "Miranda, you first."

"It's not my fault!" she began, "Emilio and I were messaging about catching up. I may have said I was psychic and that I got a message from the spirit world about some lost item. He said, 'You're not psychic.' I said, 'I am too.' He said, 'Prove it!' I said, 'I know where the diary is and nobody else does.' He said I was lying. I said, 'No, I'm not!' He said, 'Prove it then!' So, I took the diary only to prove I wasn't lying and show him I am psychic," Miranda declared.

I took a very deep breath, waited a few seconds and then asked, "So, what happened?"

"When I got to Tilly's Tea House, I saw April sitting at another table. She called me over before I had a chance to look for Emilio in the cafe. April asked me to pop outside quickly so she could show me the new car her dad had given her for her 18th birthday."

"Did you meet Emilio?" I asked, struggling to hide my displeasure.

"While she was with April," Melody continued, "I went inside Tilly's Tea House and met Emilio. I remembered he'd never met me and didn't realise we were identical twins. After Miranda left the house, I quickly found the leather diary you'd been given for Christmas. I discovered you'd only made a few entries, so I ripped them out."

"Thanks," I said, trying not to be too annoyed.

"Sorry, I still have them if you want them," Melody continued.

"Did you give him the empty diary?" I asked.

"No, I made up a few entries for each section. I then met with Emilio, who, I may add, didn't suspect a thing," Melody said triumphantly. "Oh, by the way, Miranda, he thinks you're catching up Thursday afternoon," she added.

"Thanks," Miranda said, more interested in hearing the rest of the story.

"So, what happened?" I asked, feeling slightly less anxious.

"Oh, right. Emilio was getting antsy about seeing the diary. I kept trying to put him off. I did insist I was psychic, though. I did you proud, Miranda."

"Thanks," Miranda said, smirking. Then she and I asked at the same time, "So, what happened?"

"Right, eventually I decided to take out Mum's diary and showed it to him."

"What did he say about the diary?" I asked, intrigued by the unfolding of events.

"He said, 'That doesn't mean you're psychic. It means you have a diary. Prove that it's the secret lost diary,' " Melody quoted.

"Did you show him the contents?" Miranda asked, highly amused.

"Yes, I slowly opened the diary to the pages I'd written in."

"What did he say?" Miranda asked, captivated by Melody's stand-in role.

"As he was picking up his phone, he asked if he could take a photo."

"What did you say?" I asked.

I said, "No, I'd made a promise to you that I wouldn't show anyone."

"What did he say?" Miranda asked, just beating me.

"He looked distraught and then suddenly changed his tune. He started fumbling around in his bag, then put some papers on the table on top of the diary. He became animated, explaining something about what he was studying at uni. I didn't understand a word of what he said. I just nodded. Without warning, he jumped up, grabbed all the papers off the table, made some lame excuse and ran out the door."

"So, what happened to my new Christmas diary?" I asked with that all too familiar sinking feeling in my stomach.

"Well, that's just it," Melody said. "Sorry, Mum, he took your diary with him."

"But the good news is... One, I kept your entries. They're on your bed, and two, we still have the original diary. Don't we, Miranda?"

"Umm, yes, here it is," she said embarrassed, looking down.

"Just out of curiosity, what did you write in the diary?" I said, totally bewildered at the turn of events.

"Oh, that was easy. Last week in our Practical Life Skills class, we'd been taught about morals and ethics. They gave us a sheet to study. I just copied five I thought may be relevant," Melody said proudly.

Incredibly relieved, I fell asleep with the original diary next to my bed, completely oblivious to the drastic effect it would have on the rest of my life.

CHAPTER 20

MONDAY—TWO WEEKS LATER

A s I walked into the Queens Lane Coffee House in Oxford, I was surprised to see Ruben sitting at a table. I was ten minutes early and instantly wondered if something was wrong.

Giving Ruben a big hug, I asked, "Are you OK? You're never on time, let alone early?"

Smiling broadly, he said, "Yes, everything is fine. I'm just getting better at managing my time. I decided to rearrange my priorities; you come way before any unsolicited sales call. I ended the call quickly and came straight here to see you."

I was touched by his thoughtful gesture.

"How's everything with you?" Ruben asked with that familiar kindness in his eyes.

"Really well," I said. "Interestingly, my life has suddenly started to take off."

"In what way?" Ruben asked whilst taking off his heavy jumper.

"Well, as soon as I started being more conscious and sensitive to my environment, I instantly understood my communication habits or lack of Communication Intelligence. It was like I was staring at a stage, watching a drama unfold," I explained.

"What do you do differently?" Ruben asked, intrigued by my transformation.

"I started by being more observant of time and space," I elaborated. "Before launching into a conversation, I'd consider whether it was a good time to speak, not only for me but also for my audience. I now think about the best medium to have a conversation. On many occasions, digital communication is the fastest and most convenient but least fruitful method. I'm now aware of my mood and the mood of the person I'm talking to as well as being conscious of the right time and place to chat. I'm also conscious of asking sensitive questions rather than dominating a conversation. I suppose you could say I have a heightened sense of scanning for feedback from the recipient of my communication."

"What do you do with this feedback?" Ruben said, smiling broadly at my newfound wisdom.

"I suppose it allows me to take control and steer the conversation in a more productive direction and avoid an emotional collision course," I said, pausing to make sense of my changes.

"How is it different from your old way of communicating?"

"To be honest, I've gained true Communication Intelligence. Taking the time to be aware and conscious has had an enormous impact on my empathetic ability. This, in turn, has opened my eyes to a whole new world of information."

"What sort of information?"

"Information that's always been there, right before my eyes, including environmental cues, body language, signs and symbols. I just didn't know how to recognise or interpret them," I explained.

"Has it taken long to make these changes to your communication habits?" Ruben asked curious yet slightly sceptical.

"No, actually, it's amazing how quickly you can change when you have a different point of view," I explained. "The key is being willing to open your eyes and acknowledge the information and cues staring you in the face. The doorway to success is translating this information into knowledge you can use to create stronger connections and improved relationships."

"Sounds profound. In what way has your life started to take off?" Ruben enquired, raising his right eyebrow.

"For starters, my relationship with the girls is much deeper and more respectful. Let's face it—they are very headstrong, determined young ladies. We now enter conversations more sensitively and less like a bull at a gate. Even Miranda has come a long way. We ask more questions and make fewer assumptions. You could say we speak with clarity. When we ask the other person to do something we always tell them why. This way we avoid uncertainty as to what we really mean. When we disagree instead of arguing we ask questions to uncover what the other persons means, and repeat back to make sure we understood."

"Have you made up your mind about Milan?" he asked whilst stealing a chip off my plate.

"Yes, after a lot of deliberation and speaking to the girls, I've decided to take the job. It means I'll fly to Milan once a week for meetings until September."

"How do you feel about that?" Ruben asked with the skill and expertise of a Communication Intelligence professional.

"Really excited and ready for a change." I smiled. Our time in St Moritz helped me heal. Wellbeing centres may heal physical trauma, but there's no better healing than sincere friendship and a healthy dose of self-honesty." I called over a waiter to order another bowl of chips and then turned to Ruben and asked, "What about you? How was Australia?"

"It was wonderful to be back home. I also used the information we learnt from the diary. I discovered Sarah and I aren't on different pages, after all," Ruben said thoughtfully. "We don't want different things; we just didn't fully understand each other or our priorities."

"So, what are you going to do about work? Will you stay in Rotterdam?" I asked.

"I've spoken to Isaac," Ruben said. "He said I can work remotely. Meaning, I'll be based in Australia, travelling to Rotterdam once a month for approximately a week to ten days. So not too dissimilar to you."

"When do you start?" I asked, sad that we'd be so far apart.

"I'll make the transition in the next month," he said, looking down into his coffee. "Don't worry; we can still meet up he said, resting his hand on mine. I'll be flying here regularly, and Milan is part of my region, so we can explore together."

"That would be so much fun. Will you be changing roles?" I asked.

"Not really. Rissy, stop keeping me in suspense. Did you bring the diary?" he asked, irked by my continual questions.

"Yes, I did," I said, slowly handing him the leather-bound diary.

There was a very long pause as he turned it over several times and stroked the leather. "This is incredible, just as I imagined. What an amazing piece of history we hold in our hands."

"Yes, and how easily we almost lost it," I said, ashamed and embarrassed by Miranda's impulsive behaviour.

"Can you imagine if Hans Bokman Jr. had got hold of it before anyone else had a chance even to read it," Ruben said aghast.

"I forgot to tell you the latest gossip I heard about Hans Bokman Jr.," I said, suddenly sitting bolt upright.

"What's happened now?" he asked, trying not to sound too shocked.

"Well, remember my friend Margaret Brown? She said she'd heard from a very accurate source that he's been charged with some sort of cyber espionage."

"What does that mean?" Ruben asked.

"Apparently, through the dashboard of his industrial waste purification system, he could infiltrate computer systems. He used a 'trojan' technique to steal data. He paid criminals from the dark web to hack into and crash his clients' computers."

"What did they do with the stolen data and crashed computers?" Ruben asked, confused.

"The cybercriminals held the data to ransom until the client paid an amount in bitcoins to unlock their computer and then released the data," I said, trying to sound digitally intelligent.

"That's unbelievable. Thank goodness Hans Jr. didn't get hold of the diary; it would be all through the dark web by now," Ruben said, appalled. Then he asked, "Have you had a chance to read the entire diary yet? Do you know how all the sections weave together?"

"I have. In fact, I've just come back from Italy."

"Why Italy?"

"I was unsure what to do next and whether I was on the right track. As much as I like Tina Bokman, I didn't think it was wise to go back to her. Instead, I asked Frieda if she could help me."

"What did she say?" Ruben asked, shocked I'd actually asked someone for help.

"Firstly, I went to Milan to sign my new contract. Then I popped down to Lake Como to see Frieda," I said, deliberately stalling.

"And?" Ruben asked.

"I asked Frieda if she'd be my mentor. She kindly put two days aside in her busy diary to slowly go through each section until I had a clear grasp of each principle," I explained.

"Can you give me a summary?" Ruben asked.

"Yes, she started by asking me how my world had changed since learning about the different sections."

"What did you say?" Ruben asked.

"I told her what I'd just told you, by slowing down and utilising the power of awareness and empathy, it had given me a new level of sensitivity towards others, which in turn created much deeper relationships."

"So, what else did Frieda say about the diary?" Ruben asked still flicking through the diary. "Was there a section at the back that we hadn't seen?"

"Yes, the diary ends by describing a Communication Evolution," I replied.

"How does that work?" he asked.

"When a critical mass achieves a competent level of Communication Intelligence, the world will enter a communication evolution never before experienced by humanity," I recounted.

"That's quite an assertion," Ruben said, clearly doubting the enormity of the statement.

"That's what I thought; however, Frieda went on to clarify what took effect in Westerbork."

"Go on." Ruben raised an eyebrow.

"Frieda said while they were in the camp, they created a micro Communication Evolution using the principles of Communication Intelligence. She explained that upon arrival into the camp, every prisoner was stripped not only of their personal belongings but also of their persona, their belief systems and values. Hierarchies vanished when job titles were removed being replaced only by survival skills."

"How did they create a Communication Evolution?"

"It began through the dedication of the men and women in the secret meetings. They used the principles proven by their studies and data analysis to teach Communication Intelligence."

"I'm still confused," Ruben said with a shake of his head. "It seems hard to believe the authors of the diary gained all this incredible knowledge whilst stuck in a camp surrounded by the atrocities inflicted by the Nazis."

"I know," I replied. "The same thoughts ran through my head. Frieda said the methods of psychological warfare used by the Nazis were analysed and passionately debated. Many of the prisoners had been prominent in their fields of expertise before entering the camp. They could smuggle letters in and out of the camp to help with their research and communication strategy. They were fortunate to get access to some of the most current field research at the time."

"How did they influence the entire culture within the camp?" Ruben asked.

"David Solomon and his team recognised the camp's culture amounted to the social behaviour of the entire group of prisoners within this enclosed environment," I explained. "It was a unique situation allowing them to study the impact of Crowd Psychology, Awareness, Empathy, Interaction, Observation of time and space and conscious Understanding," I relayed just as Frieda had told me.

"Arriving in the camp was an instant culture shock to the prisoners. First, they had to come to terms with desolating new social norms, insurmountable fear and immense issues of distrust. Next, they had to work out the best way to communicate with other prisoners, whilst being under constant surveillance. They quickly worked out:

'The most important thing in communication is to hear what isn't being said.'

The Nazis were very cunning. They didn't select which prisoners would go on the trains; instead, they instructed designated prisoners to make the decision. They created a situation of Jew against Jew, to promote anarchy, and hatred within the camp."

"I had no idea this happened," Ruben said, shocked. "How did the prisoners manage the culture with such appalling decision-making placed upon them?"

"This is the basis of the diary. It began with 'Awareness' and acceptance. The prisoners had to be fully aware of the environment they were living in, aware of who they could and couldn't trust. They had to watch patterns and learn new systems. Then they had to look at themselves and determine their priorities. They found higher meaning when they were clear on who they were beyond their status and job title. This truth set their minds free," I explained. "Once the prisoners become conscious and sensitive to their environment, they had to be willing to fully embrace the principle of empathy which allowed them to truly connect with others. This meant being willing to not only receive information but give honest feedback."

"How did the prisoners mentally deal with the pure evil of the Nazis guards?" Ruben asked.

"Frieda said that this was one of the most challenging hurdles the prisoners had to confront," I stated. "The writers of the diary cautiously placed constant reminders throughout the camp in the form of secret signs and symbols, that said: *'When you fight the dragon, you become the dragon.'* " I paused to take a sip of my coffee, then continued: "So, the real secret to the Communication Evolution within the camp was leading by example. The principle of Interaction, in particular the power of reciprocity, cannot be overstressed. They also found: *'The more we say, the less people remember.'* "

"How did the principle of observing time and space affect the prisoners and their culture?" Ruben asked, clearly fascinated by how much he was learning.

"The prisoners constantly listened and watched for cues, to understand when and where was the best time and place to communicate out of the watchful eyes of the guards. It may have been a change of shift, during bad weather, or a commotion in the camp. The prisoners who survived best were masters of 'stop, look and listen.'"

"My guess is they had also mastered the last principle of conscious understanding," Ruben added.

I nodded. "Yes, Frieda said that when the camp was liberated, the most successful and later prosperous prisoners both within the camp and subsequently after the war displayed the strongest signs of conscious understanding. The principles of Awareness, Empathy, Interaction, Observation and Understanding had become second nature to them. What was also very interesting;

these prisoners suffered less from mental health issues than those who had not embraced the principles. That was their Communication Evolution."

"That's very interesting, especially about the mental health issues," Ruben said, "but you still haven't told me about the last part of the diary. What does it say about tying all the principles together to make it so powerful?"

"If you look at the second half of the diary, it becomes an instruction manual for corporate training and work-shops," I explained. "It says the five principles are like baking a chocolate cake. Anyone can have the separate ingredients in their cupboard or bought in a box. However, to create a cake that rises and tastes sensational, you need to measure the correct amount of each ingredient, place the ingredients in a bowl in the correct order, stirred for the right amount of time and place it in the oven at the most appropriate temperature for the correct amount of time. That's when you achieve the best results."

"That makes a lot of sense," Ruben said. "Where do you go from here?"

"Very good question." I smiled. "Frieda is part of the elder's group trying to block the release of the diary. I asked if I could attend their next meeting to see if I could change their mind about communicating the contents to the world in a controlled manner."

"Have you done this?" he asked, slightly annoyed he'd missed all these details while he was in Australia.

"Yes, sorry. While I was in Lake Como with Frieda, she mentioned she was going to Davos that evening to meet the elders. She rang the chairperson and got permission for me to attend as a guest."

"What happened?" Ruben asked.

"There were three other survivors of the concentration camps, who were adamant the contents should never be released," I explained. "I did my best to convince them the world had changed considerably since the Second World War."

"Did you manage to convince them?" Ruben asked, anxious to hear the outcome.

"I think the turning point came when we discussed the digital revolution," I continued, "including the effects of artificial intelligence and the impact on the millennial generation who are ready to accelerate the process of the Fourth Dimension in Communication. I told them this generation is the most educated generation in history. They already have a sense that something is missing. It's time to end society's tunnel vision and respect and trust this new generation."

"Did you manage to convince them to release the contents of the diary?" Ruben asked.

"Yes, but they stipulated conditions," I replied.

"What were they?"

"It was agreed we could set up the 'Communication Intelligence Academy' with the help of Frieda. We would be required to have a board with at least two elders, one of them being Frieda. The academy would teach the contents outlined in the diary and create licenced Practitioners in Communication Intelligence. The practitioners would become experts in the five principles transforming information into knowledge which would help adapt behaviours in commercial landscapes. The practitioners would focus on rehumanising communication to embrace the whole-mind, whole-body and whole-system to create a wholly unique interactive experience."

"Congratulations, Rissy. I am so proud of you," Ruben said, trying hard to hide the tears welling in his eyes. "You are definitely out of the darkness. Your grandparents would be so proud."

"I know," I said. "I remember one of the last words my grandmother said to me. *'It is possible to live happily ever after but remember it's on a moment-to-moment basis.'*"

FIVE PRINCIPLES
TO RAISE
COMMUNICATION
INTELLIGENCE

PRINCIPLE 1   AWARENESS OF SELF,
               LISTENER, ENVIRONMENT

PRINCIPLE 2   EMPATHY—CONNECT TO
               YOUR AUDIENCE

PRINCIPLE 3   INTERACT FOLLOWING
               LAWS OF PULL AND PUSH

PRINCIPLE 4   OBSERVE TIME AND SPACE

PRINCIPLE 5   UNDERSTAND YOU HAVE
               A CHOICE

Communication Intelligence = (AO+UE) X I

You gain *Communication Intelligence* when you combine Awareness and Observation together with Understanding Empathy which is applied to Interaction

Awareness—Once humankind is aware of their feelings, thoughts and actions and how they affect others, they will be able to successfully engage with everyone no matter what their background or personality type. Awareness will remove people's resistance to ideas and help create more creative solutions.

'If you plant poison ivy, you won't harvest strawberries.'

Empathy—Communication is about connection. Effective communication requires understanding how to connect with the listener. Asking the right type of question in the right order improves empathy in communication.

'People won't remember what you said, but they will remember how you made them feel.'

Interaction—People tend to react in predictable ways, according to the laws of human relations. Everyone is affected by the push and pull when interacting with others. Understanding the basics such as reciprocity, congruency, likability, authority and group psychology is the basis for Communication Intelligence.

'The more we say, the less people remember.'

Observation—Time and Space—Between every action and reaction, there is a space. In that space, you have the power to choose your response and the time to respond.

'Time is your most precious commodity, and it is non-renewable. Respect other people's time.'

Understanding—Conscious understanding—We cannot always control our circumstances, but we can and do choose our response to whatever arises. You have the choice to drift along or make conscious decisions.

'My destination is no longer a location but a new way of conscious understanding.'

SIX MONTHS LATER

Lulu, the fish, has survived two more operations, and her lump has been reduced by half.

Melody accepted her offer to study at the Royal Veterinary College.

Miranda accepted her offer from Oxford to study law.

Stewit the rabbit has been banned from free movement in the living room.

Ruben, Sarah and the kids have just returned from the Great Barrier Reef and found a new depth to their relationship.

Hans Bokman Jr. is living at Her Majesty's pleasure. His new business 'Prisonway' has proved a phenomenal success with his captive audience.

Emilio, after reading Melody's 'insights' in the fake diary, realised the error of his ways and has decided not to follow in his father's footsteps. He sheepishly returned the diary to Miranda.

Miranda and Emilio are now an item.

Tina Bokman is loving seeing more of Emilio and Miranda and hearing all their stories.

Frieda has excelled in her role as a mentor.

Iris and Fabrizio have spent many hours sailing into the sunset, getting to know each other better.

ACKNOWLEDGEMENT

Thank you for taking the time to read this book. I hope the ideas and insights help you as much as they have helped me and countless others along my path. I hope it has as much impact on your life as it has on mine to catapult you to new levels of success and effectiveness in communication.

Communication is a vast field with many influencing factors. There isn't enough time or space to cover all elements of communication within these covers, so I focused on what I believe to be five major factors in Communication Intelligence and the Fourth Dimension in Communication. I have personally lived and experienced first-hand all the ideas mentioned in this book. My life has taken many twists and turns, and I've learned to climb many mountains without a safety harness. I have fallen more times than I can remember and learned to brush myself off and just find another way. Life threw me a few nasty curveballs, and I just had to get on with it. Giving up was never an option.

I dedicate this book to my loving grandparents Adrian and Bertha Van As, who were based in Camp Westerbork from 1942-1945. They were awarded a Righteous Gentile Certificate in 1992 for saving lives during their time in the camp. This book does not claim to be an accurate account of facts and events that took place in the camp. It is a dedication to the suffering of all people who endured the horrendous psychological warfare of the Nazis and to highlight the millions of unrecorded and unknown victims.

The ideas and insights you have read are based on proven scientific techniques. The Lost Art of Communication Intelligence is a paradigm shift in examining communication from a new dimension, taking into consideration verbal and nonverbal communication, including the surrounding environment and time, place, and space.

I hope my contribution to the field of communication will create better understanding and deeper relationships. I aim to enhance career prospects, improve corporate culture and make seismic shifts in the new corporate landscape.

I'm a lover of knowledge and new ideas. Every concept I present I have personally tried out in my work and personal life. I have immersed myself in behavioural science for over twenty years, including gaining a Masters in Behavioural Decision Science. I have also worked as a lawyer and as a Chief Compliance Officer, and Chief Behavioural Officer.

As a disclaimer, the wise and insightful contributions throughout this book should be credited to the experts who have preceded me and who I acknowledge throughout this book. Like a master chef, I have simply used the various ingredients in the correct order and the right amount to come up with a new recipe.

SOURCES

The inspiration and wisdom for this story came from the following readings:

Benedict, Elsie Lincoln & Ralph Paine Benedict, *How to Analyse People On Sight: Through the Science of Human Analysis: The Five Human Types,* New York, e-artnow (10 Nov. 2013)

Bolton, Robert, *People Skills: How to Assert Yourself, Listen to Others, And Resolve Conflict,* New York: Simon & Schuster Inc, 1979

Charvet, Shelle Rose, *Words That Change Minds: The 14 Patterns For Mastering The Language of Influence*, Institute for Influence; 3rd edition (22 Mar. 2019)

Cialdini, Robert, *Influence: The Psychology of Persuasion*, New York: Harper Collins, 2007

Coyle, Daniel, *The Culture Code: The Secrets to Highly Successful Groups*, Random House Business, 2019

Crabbe, Tony, *Busy: How to Thrive in a World of Too Much,* Great Britain: Piatkus, 2015

Daugherty, Paul R., Wilson, H. James, *Human + Machine: Reimaging Work in the Age of AI*, Boston: Harvard Business Review Press, 2018

Dimitrius, Jo-Ellen & Mark Mazzarella, *Reading People*, London: Random House, 1998

Einstein, Albert, *The World as I See It; Einstein's views on Life, Science & Human Nature*, CreateSpace Independent Publishing Platform, 2014

Frankl, Viktor E., *Man's Search for Meaning*, London: Random House, 1959

Gallagher, Winifred, *The Power of Place: How Our Surroudings Shape Our Thoughts, Emotions, And Actions*, New York, Simon & Schuster, 1993

Gladwell, Malcolm, *The Tipping Point: How Little Things Can Make a Big Difference*, Great Britain: Abacus 2000

Gracian, Baltasar, Translated by Joseph Jacobs, *The Art of Worldly Wisdom*, London: MacMillan and Co, 1892

Greene, Robert, *The Laws of Human Nature: The 48 Laws of Power*, Great Britain: Profile Books, 2018

Hall, Edward T. *The Hidden Dimension*, New York Bantam Doubleday Dell Publishing Group; 1988

Hall, Edward T. *The Silent Language*, New York, Bantam Doubleday Dell Publishing Group; Reissue 1973

Infante, Dominic A. Andrew W. Rancer, Deanna F. Womack, *Building Communication Theory*, Illinois: Waveland Press, Inc, 2003

Kershaw, Ian, *The 'Hitler Myth'*, Oxford University Press, 1987

Krznaric, Roman, *Empathy: Why it Matters and How To Get It*, Great Britain: Rider, Random House, 2015

Le Bon, Gustave, *The Crowd; Study of the Popular Mind*, Dover Publications Inc.; Reprint edition, 2003

Lewrick, Michael, Patrick Link, Larry Leifer, *The Design Thinking Toolbox: A Guide to Mastering the Most Popular and Valuable Innovation Methods*, New Jersey: John Wiley & Sons, Inc, 2020

Nirenberg, Jesse S., *Breaking Through to Each Other,* New York: Harper & Row, 1976

Marquet, L. David and Steve R. Covey: *Turn the Ship Around: A True Story of Turning Followers into Leaders*, Penguin, 2015

Marrs, Jim *Ruled by Secrecy*, New York: Haper Collins, 2000

Mayfield, Anthony, *Me and My Web Shadow: How to Manage Your Reputation Online,* Great Britain: A&C Black Publishers Ltd, 2010

Montes, Javier, *Millennial Workforce: Cracking the Code to Generation Y In Your Company*, Lulu Publishing, 2017

Mortensen, C. David, *Communication: The Study of Human Interaction*, USA, McGraw Hill Higher Education, 1972

Nichols, Michael P., *The Lost Art of Listening: How Learning to Listen Can Improve Relationships,* New York, London: The Guildford Press, 2009

Harari, Yuval Noah, *Sapiens: A Brief History of Humankind*, Great Britain: Penguin Random House, 2015

O'Connell, Mark, and Raje Airey, *Signs & Symbols: Identification and analysis of the visual vocabulary that formulates our thoughts and dictates our reactions to the world around us*, Lorenz Books, 2005

Orme, Greg, *The Human Edge: How Curiosity and Creativity Are Your Superpowers in The Digital Economy*, Harlow England: Pearson Education Limited, 2019

Parise, Eli, *The Filter Bubble: What the Internet Is Hiding from You*, Penguin, 2012

Rosenberg, Marshall B., *Nonviolent Communication: A Language of Life*, PuddleDancer Press, 2015

Scheflen, Albert E. & Norman Ashcraft, *Human Territories: How We Behave In Space-Time*, New Jersey, Prentice Hall Inc, 1976

Smith, Clagett G., *Conflict Resolution; Contributions of the Behavioural Sciences*, University of Notre Dame Press, Indiana, 1971

Stein, Alexander, *Terror, Love and Brainwashing: Attachment in Cults and Totalitarian Systems*, London and New York: Routledge, 2017

Maria Stuart, Maria & Gary Scott Lively, *Communication Nonverbal: How Reading Nonverbal Communication Can Help You Win At Life*, ambracom (1 Nov. 2020)

Tegmark, Max, *Life 3.0; Being Human in the Age of Artificial Intelligence*, Penguin; 2018

Tiede, Bob, *Now That's a Great Question*, e-publishing

Immins, Lois Ed. D, *Understanding Through Communication: Structured Experiments in Self-Exploration*, Illinois, U.S.A, Charles C. Thomas, 1972

Unver, Burhan *Rumi Quotes*, independently published, 2019

Van Ruler, Betteke, Frank Korver, *The Communication Strategy Handbook: Toolkit for Creating Winning Strategy*, New York: Peter Lang Publishing, 2019

Van As, Adrian, *In the Lion's Den*, Victoria: Makor Jewish Community Library, 2012

Wenger, Win & Richard Poe, *The Einstein Factor*, New York: Three Rivers Press, 1995

Willems, Eddy, *Cyberdanger: Understanding and Guarding Against Cybercrime*, Switzerland: Springer, 2013

Young, Gary, *Ethics In the Virtual World: The Morality and Psychology of Gaming*, Great Britain: Acumen, 2013